HOW TO USE A BOOK AS A MARKETING
& INCOME ACCELERATOR

PUBLISH
A BOOK & GROW RICH

PLAN IT | WRITE IT | PUBLISH IT | FUND IT | MOVE IT

GERRY ROBERT

Copyright © MMXVII Gerry Robert

ALL RIGHTS RESERVED. No part of this book may be reproduced or transmitted in any form whatsoever, electronic, or mechanical, including photocopying, recording, or by any informational storage or retrieval system without the expressed written, dated and signed permission from the author.

Author: Gerry Robert
Title: Publish a Book & Grow Rich
ISBN: 978-1-77204-546-8
Category: MARKETING/Branding/Entrepreneurship/Sales

Publisher: Black Card Books
Division of Gerry Robert Enterprises Inc.
Suite 214, 5-18 Ringwood Dr.
Stouffville, Ontario Canada, L4A 0N2
International Calling: +1 877 280 8536
www.blackcardbooks.com
Gerry's Cover Photo: © David McCammon

POWERED BY
black card
BOOKS

LIMITS OF LIABILITY/DISCLAIMER OF WARRANTY: The author and publisher of this book have used their best efforts in preparing this material. The author and publisher make no representation or warranties with respect to the accuracy, applicability or completeness of the contents. They disclaim any warranties (expressed or implied), or merchantability for any particular purpose. No portion of this material is intended to offer legal, professional, personal or financial advice. The information contained herein cannot replace or substitute for the services of trained professionals in any field, including, but not limited to, financial or legal matters.

Under no circumstances will Gerry Robert or Gerry Robert Enterprises Inc., or any of its divisions such as Black Card Books, or any of its representatives or contractors be liable for any loss or other damages, including but not limited to special, incidental, consequential, or other damages. The information presented in this publication is compiled from sources believed to be accurate, however, the publisher assumes no responsibility for errors or omissions. The information in this publication is not intended to replace or substitute professional advice. The author and publisher specifically disclaim any liability, loss, or risk that is incurred as a consequence, directly or indirectly, of the use and application of any of the contents of this work. You alone are responsible and accountable for your decisions, actions and results in life, and by your use of the information presented herein, you agree not to attempt to hold the author or publisher liable for any such decisions, actions or results at any time, under any circumstance.

The author and publisher have taken every effort to ensure we accurately represent these strategies and their potential to help you grow your business. However, the author and publisher do not purport this as a "get-rich scheme" and there is no guarantee that you will earn any money using the techniques displayed here. Your level of success in attaining similar results is dependent upon a number of factors, including your skill, knowledge, ability, dedication, personality, market, business savvy, business focus, business goals, partners, and financial situation. Because these factors differ according to individuals, the author and publisher cannot guarantee your success, income level, or ability to earn revenue.

Any forward-looking or financial statements outlined here are simply expectations or forecasts for future potential, and are thus not promises for actual performance. These statements are simply based on opinion or experience. As stipulated by law, no future guarantees can be made that you will achieve any results from the information in this book, and the author and publisher offer no professional legal or financial advice.

Library and Archives Canada Cataloguing in Publication.

Robert, Gerry, 1958-

Printed in Canada

HOW TO USE A BOOK AS A MARKETING TOOL
& INCOME ACCELERATOR

PUBLISH A BOOK & GROW RICH

PLAN IT | WRITE IT | PUBLISH IT | FUND IT | MOVE IT

GERRY ROBERT

Other books by Gerry Robert:

Conquering Life's Obstacles
The Magic of Real Estate
A Tale of Two Websites
The Millionaire Mindset
Multiply Your Business

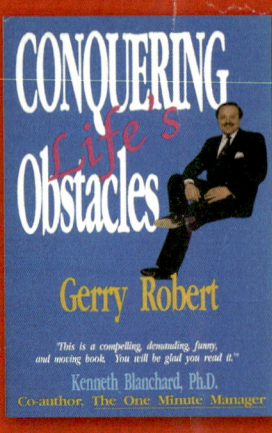 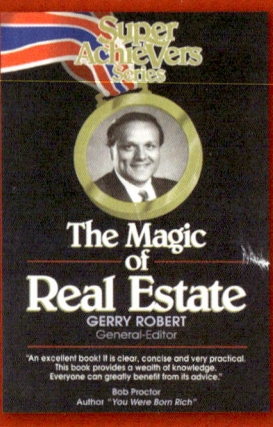 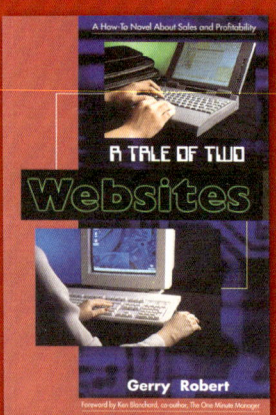 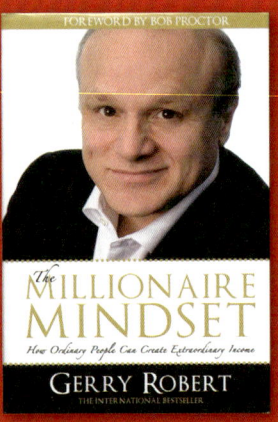 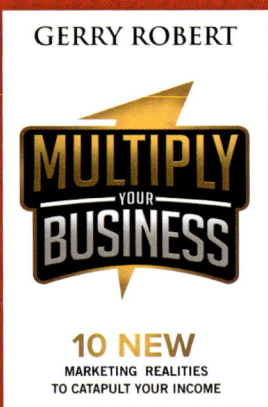

Testimonials

"Being in the car business, I've been exposed to the best of the best in terms of speakers and trainers. Gerry is by far one of the top ones. This book gives you EVERYTHING you need to publish and grow rich."

Allan Lorraine
Author of *Sales Manager Reset*

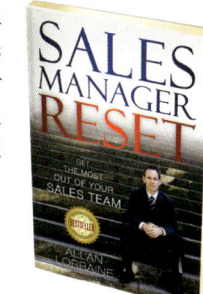

"Real estate agents the world over love this book because competition is so massive today and this book provides the cutting-edge marketing solutions for anyone wanting to grow their practice."

Theresa Barnabei, DREC
Co-author of *Multiply Your Business*

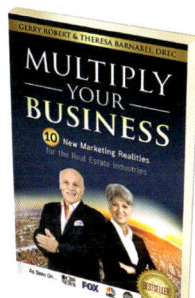

"I was shocked when I read this book and how much Gerry gives in it. The entire roadmap on how to use a book as a marketing tool is revealed. No wonder he brings in tens upon tens of millions per year. Anyone who is serious about building a coaching practice should follow this book's wisdom."

Kevin Judge
Author of *How to Fix a Bad Boss*

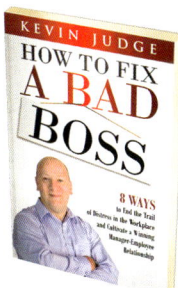

Shirley Anthony

Author of *The NEW Entrepreneur*
Marketing Consultant, Marketing Breakthroughs

Email: shirley@marbreak.co.za
Website: www.marbreak.co.za
Send an email to info@marbreak.co.za to arrange a FREE marketing consulting session with me via Skype.

What is your Primary Objective?
My book opens doors for me to speak in front of and train would-be entrepreneurs and business owners on how to launch, sustain and grow their businesses.

What has been your biggest win?
My book launch in March 2015. I have had over 20 media reviews of my book and undertaken four radio interviews. I have launched a new Marketing Mentor product in my business and I have just had my first corporate sign up for this program.

What has been your experience working with Gerry Robert?
I have found the Black Card Books Instant Author Program to be very professional and the team 100% supportive. I really felt as though I had people holding my hand throughout the writing, editing and publishing process. Nothing was ever too much for this team and my book was published and printed within nine months of signing up for the program!

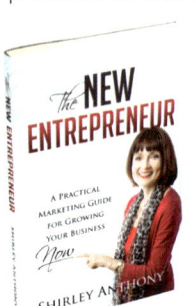

Do you recommend the Publish a Book & Grow Rich bootcamp?
Yes, the best publishing seminar ever!

Bathandwa (Nombasa) Mcuba

Author of *Creative Culture*
Arts and Culture Consultant

Email: bathandwa@theafricanshow.com
Website: www.creativeculture31.com
Visit my website to download your FREE copy of my book.

What is your Primary Objective?
To launch my business and position myself as an authority in my field. I want to travel, open doors and meet influential people so that I can create awareness and educate others through speaking and writing.

What has been your biggest win?
Traveling the world and having the income from Creative Culture take care of all the expenses. It's awesome!

What has been your experience working with Gerry Robert?
The best ever!

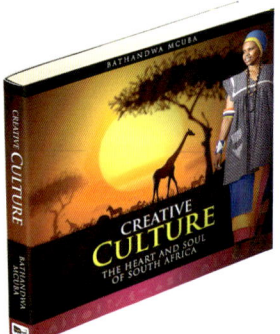

Do you recommend the Publish a Book & Grow Rich bootcamp?
I went to a class in Johannesburg. It was a crowd of hundreds upon hundreds, but I felt they were speaking directly to me. It taught me to believe in myself. Get to a class – that's my recommendation.

Rudi Zimmerer

Author of *Enjoy Your Life Now!*
Meditation Master, Therapist, Author

Email: rudi.zimmerer@gmail.com
Website: www.ask-rudy.com
Visit my website for your FREE meditation course.

What is your Primary Objective?
To spread my knowledge of meditation and personal growth to a wider audience and bring my career as a meditation teacher and therapist to new heights.

What has been your biggest win?
I've gained confidence and shared my message with more people than ever before.

What has been your experience working with Gerry Robert?
We're off to a great start! I can't wait to see what happens next with my book.

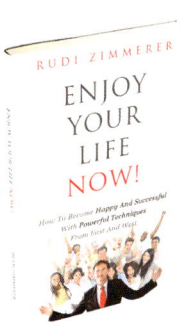

Do you recommend the Publish a Book & Grow Rich bootcamp?
I went to a class in Bangkok and it was such fun and so insightful.

Sharon Woo

Author of *Secrets Of The Financially FREE*
Business Author, Speaker, Consultant

Email: sharonwoo17@gmail.com
Website: www.secretsofthefinanciallyfree.com
Like my Facebook page "Secrets of the Financially Free" by visiting www.bit.ly/SharonWoo_FB and receive a FREE motivational poster.

What is your Primary Objective?
To become a successful platform speaker and consultant on how to achieve financial freedom.

What has been your biggest win?
Speaking at several seminars on the concept of achieving financial freedom.

What has been your experience working with Gerry Robert?
Gerry and the entire team at Black Card Books have been nothing short of exceptional! I'm impressed with the level of professionalism demonstrated by every single person I've worked with. Kudos on building a world-class support team, Gerry!

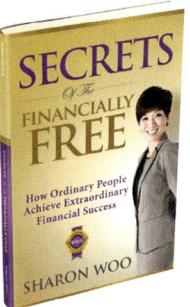

Do you recommend the Publish a Book & Grow Rich bootcamp?
I'm so happy I attended this class. I have told so many people about it. It's so much more than a publishing seminar.

Peter Ong

Author of *The Bullettrain Entrepreneur*
Author, Speaker, Entrepreneurial Coach

Email: sbm5@sbmtrain.com
Website: www.thebullettrain31.com
Visit my website to receive a FREE one-hour coaching session on my Million Dollar Model.

What is your Primary Objective?
The primary objective of my book is to establish authority, credibility and visibility as an entrepreneur, author, speaker and coach. In so doing, my revenue will increase substantially.

What has been your biggest win?
Being invited as a speaker in local and international SME conferences. I've been to the National Conference of Entrepreneurship 2015, the ASEAN SME Partnership Conference in Indonesia, and the Pan Pacific Business Conference in Vietnam.

What has been your experience working with Gerry Robert?
My experience working with Gerry Robert and his sharp, caring, results-oriented team has been amazing! My dream of becoming an author is now a reality, thanks to *Publish a Book & Grow Rich*.

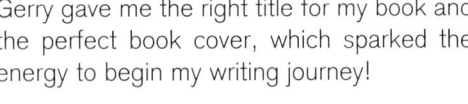

Gerry gave me the right title for my book and the perfect book cover, which sparked the energy to begin my writing journey!

Do you recommend the Publish a Book & Grow Rich bootcamp?
Yes. Just GO!

Jeffrey Grinel

Author of *RockUrBrain – Fun Memory Game*
Author, Speaker, Trainer

Email: jeffgrinel@yahoo.com
Website: www.RockUrBrain.com/FREE
Visit my website to download a FREE copy of my book.

What is your Primary Objective?
To build out a lead list in order to market and sell my online training programs.

What has been your biggest win?
Being on radio, TV and movies.

What has been your experience working with Gerry Robert?
Gerry is the best book authoring coach in the world. My story would never have been possible if I hadn't changed my belief in what was possible. Gerry did that!

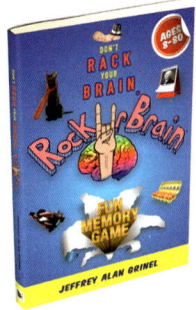

Do you recommend the Publish a Book & Grow Rich bootcamp?
They say this seminar is about books but it's really about so much more… marketing, mindset, money and more! No matter what you have to do, get yourself a ticket asap.

Jochen Siepmann

Author of *The Property Apprentice*
Author, Property Investing Trainer

Email: jochen@professionalpropertyinvestment.com
Website: www.professionalpropertyinvestment.com
Visit my website to receive a FREE property consultation worth $500.

What is your Primary Objective?
To be perceived as an expert in my field, gain authority, create better marketing and improve my brand positioning.

What has been your biggest win?
When *The Property Apprentice* was published, people began to look up to me and seek my advice on property. I got more international speaking engagements and more clients for my business than ever before.

What has been your experience working with Gerry Robert?
Awesome! Brilliant! Competent! Delightful! Educational! Fantastic! Great! Helpful! Inspiring! Joyful! Kind! Lovely! Meaningful! Nurturing! Original! Positive! Quality! Remarkable! Superb! Transformative! Unbelievable! Valuable! Wonderful! Insert infinite stream of superlatives!

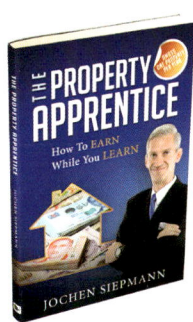

Do you recommend the Publish a Book & Grow Rich bootcamp?
I'm in the seminar business and so I've seen it all, but I was so pleasantly surprised when I attended Gerry's bootcamp. It gives a full road map to publishing and achieving your dreams.

Susie Nelsen

Author of *Finishing Well*
Author, Speaker, Realtor

Email: susienelsen@comcast.net
Website: www.susienelsen.com
Visit my website to receive a FREE copy of my book.

What is your Primary Objective?
To reach the masses with my message of encouragement and funnel new business to my team. And of course, to create a new and lucrative income stream.

What has been your biggest win?
People are so impressed with the book! Not only the message, but everything about it – the look, cover, quality, everything. It opens new doors for me everywhere I go. It's been a blast to introduce my book to local professionals! Sky's the limit!

What has been your experience working with Gerry Robert?
The team at Black Card Books is just that – a team. They were very supportive from start to finish. They were quick to offer resources and were very patient with me, all while spurring me on to keep at it.

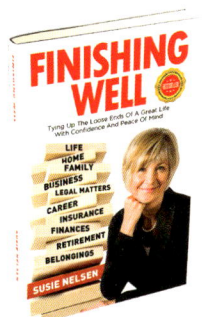

I appreciate the encouragement and positive attitudes! I know my relationship with Black Card Books is not over.

Do you recommend the Publish a Book & Grow Rich bootcamp?
Yes – without hesitation.

TESTIMONIALS

Melvin Christie

Author of *The Six C's Of Leadership*
Leadership Development

Email: mel@sixcoflesdership.com
Website: www.sixcofleadership.com
Visit my website to receive a FREE download of my book.

What is your Primary Objective?
To become a well-known, respected and premier authority on leadership!

What has been your biggest win?
I've been invited to speak at a large corporate conference. I've also been invited to address a local CEO Forum.

What has been your experience working with Gerry Robert?
I've always dreamed of writing a book. When I met Gerry, I realized from his inspirational ideas that it could actually happen. Now my dream is becoming a reality! My sincere thanks to his outstanding team. Their personal and responsive support has made all the difference.

Do you recommend the Publish a Book & Grow Rich bootcamp?
I highly recommend this workshop. I benefited from the practical information about writing and marketing my book. The insights I had during the session continue to inspire.

Sally May Tan

Author of *Wellness, The New Luxury*
Author, Speaker, Wellness Whisperer

Email: sally@wellnessthenewluxury.com
Website: www.WellnessTheNewLuxury.com
Send me an email with your health goals and receive a FREE copy of my book PLUS two hour-long coaching sessions.

What is your Primary Objective?
I aim to seal my reputation as the Wellness Coach of choice in the corporate health industry. I also aim to reach more clients, both individual corporate executives and organizations.

What has been your biggest win?
Being featured as a Nutrition Expert on the *Health Matters* program on Channel News Asia – which is Asia's largest news network! I had eight minutes of airtime. Priceless!

What has been your experience working with Gerry Robert?
Gerry and his team were there for me during the ENTIRE process of publishing my first book. Some speakers sell you something spectacular from the stage but let you down once you sign on the dotted line. Well, my book is proof that Gerry is not one of those people! His promise and method work wonders.

Do you recommend the Publish a Book & Grow Rich bootcamp?
The workshop is brilliant. Worth every penny!

Stanley Beckett

Author of *LIFTOFF*
Trainer, Coach, Author

Email: stanley@invisioncoaching.co.za
Website: www.liftoff31.com
Visit my website and receive a FREE downloadable copy of my book.

What is your Primary Objective?
The primary objective for my book is to showcase who I am and what I teach. I plan to use it as both a recruiting and influence building tool.

What has been your biggest win?
My book has opened many training opportunities, including a multi-million dollar training job.

What has been your experience working with Gerry Robert?
Gerry helped me break through the terror barrier when it came to writing this book. I struggled to open doors before I met Gerry. With his mentorship and proven training methods, I raised over $25,000 in two days. I achieved in three months what I had not been able to do in 10 years. Thank you, Gerry!

Do you recommend the Publish a Book & Grow Rich bootcamp?
This bootcamp is masterful. It gives you all you need to publish a great book.

David Bunney

Author of *Success Leaves A Trail*
Author, Speaker, Mentor

Email: mail@davidbunney.com
Website: www.davidbunney.com
Visit www.successleavesatrail.com/bonuses to receive a FREE copy of my book.

What is your Primary Objective?
The purpose of writing my book was to raise my profile to help build a brand and speaking career.

What has been your biggest win?
My biggest win is simply being associated with Black Card Books. Before the book was even published, I secured a major joint-venture partnership. After publication, my book made the Amazon Best Seller list, which raised my profile and launched my speaking career.

What has been your experience working with Gerry Robert?
The amazing Black Card Books team helped me achieve things I did not believe I could. Words cannot describe the feeling of having an experienced team behind you that believes in you, sometimes more than you believe in yourself. I am amazed at the culture of genuine helpfulness throughout the organization. Thank you, Black Card.

Do you recommend the Publish a Book & Grow Rich bootcamp?
Yes – I tell everyone about it.

Black Card Books Production Team

Acknowledgements

I would like to begin by thanking my CEO, Jean-Guy Francoeur, without whose help in running our company (Black Card Books) I would never have had the time to complete this book. His leadership in running an international company, his dedication to our customers and team is incredible. He lives to #hustle and I am truly grateful for his leadership and friendship.

Deborah Turton, the Chief Operating Officer at Black Card Books, is a rare gem of a lady. She combines sharp wit and commitment to nurture people, but also demonstrates in her life and attitude a WHATEVER IT TAKES mentality. She leads a huge team and they all love her as I do.

My son, Corey, is an integral part of our leadership team. As Director of Marketing, he is responsible for filling our bootcamps and does a masterful job for us. I so love that I get to work with him every day.

Bonnie Canesso, who heads our sales team, is also outstanding. This lady makes things happen. She is a superstar at generating revenue. She really cares about our people and our cause. I love traveling the world with her and the team of crack publishing consultants she leads.

Rodrigo Arguera is a key player in my life as head of finance for our company. He makes sure our books are stellar and at over 300% growth per year; his hands are full.

All of these people are IMPECCABLE. I couldn't do what we do to service the tens of thousands of students we reach each year, and hundreds of authors we publish, if it wasn't for all of the dedicated team members at Black Card Books. There are over 150+ on our payroll, so I can't thank them all, but I would like to acknowledge them all for caring so much for our clients and really helping make this company a family.

Speaking of the thousands upon thousands of clients we have, I would like to give a particular shout-out to members of our Revenue Sharing Deal and Mike Turton who heads that division, and also to our Instant Author Program Team. They have invested heavily in us, and they inspire me daily.

I would also like to thank Richard and Veronica Tan, and the entire team at Success Resources. They are the largest seminar providers in the world and they put me on the biggest stages with luminaries like Tony Robbins, Richard Branson, Robert Kiyosaki and others.

Lastly, I would like to share that my family blesses me so much. Anne, my wife of over 30 years, is a gem; Corey and Lindsay, Trevor and Katrina, Evan and Ivanna are simply the best. I can't believe how lucky I am that they are in my life.

Foreword

It is not often that you can be present at the birth of an industry. It's very special when you can do it twice. What's even more amazing is the fact that the same man was responsible for both events!

In April 1991, Gerry Robert and I attended an event entitled *The Million Dollar Forum*. The event was designed to help the participants take their ideas and celebrate them in the marketplace – in other words, start a new business.

Gerry Robert was one of the more notable students in the entire event for a few reasons: He was funny and contributed a lot to the class, he was extremely helpful to the other students in the room, he had an extremely simple yet revolutionary idea – and much to the amazement of all students and instructors who were present, someone funded Gerry's idea right at the event!

What first made Gerry noticeable to his fellow classmates was his overwhelming generosity. He gave every person in the room a complimentary copy of his first book, *Conquering Life's Obstacles*.

Many thoughts floated through my mind when I received my copy of Gerry's written word: Wow! How generous! Why did he do that? That must have cost him a lot! Cool! I'm jealous! I wish I could've thought of doing that! What a great idea!

That single simple gesture of giving his book away cemented in my mind my memory of Gerry – forever! Not only was I personally experiencing this nice man's philanthropy – I was witnessing the birth of an entirely new way of marketing: Using a book as a marketing tool!

The idea was so simply ingenious that one of the students shared with Gerry that they thought it was one of the most remarkable ideas that they had seen in a while and offered to fund Gerry's idea – right on the spot.

I had the good fortune to partner with Jack Canfield and Mark Victor Hansen as I became the first Canadian and first male co-author in their international bestselling book series. My book, *A Cup of Chicken Soup for the Soul*, served 580,000 souls around the world and opened up speaking opportunities from 1996 to this very day. Thankfully, I was able to blend what I learned from Jack and Mark with the marketing expertise from Gerry to expand my own personal brand. I was blessed to author 10 books in total.

Gerry spent the next few decades travelling the world and spreading the message of using a book as a marketing tool. Millions of people heard and benefitted from his message, and they implemented Gerry's ideas to achieve greater results in their businesses and professional lives by sharing their thoughts and ideas in a book.

As with all successful ideas, soon there would be imitators, copycats and the inevitable 'know-it-alls' who would profess that THEY were the ones who could change your life by using a book. Gerry ended up creating most of his competition as they would attend Gerry's events, 'borrow' his ideas and hang their shingle as a 'marketing consultant' who specialised in books.

As usual, many of the imitators quickly fell by the wayside as they realized there was more to it than repeating what they thought they knew.

In addition to the fact that a copy is never as good as the original – the primary reason the copycats did not succeed was they were always dealing with the old ideas – they never had the mindset, heart-set and work-set that came from the original visionary – Gerry Robert. By the time the 'know-it-alls' implemented their ideas, Gerry was creating new and interesting ways to enhance what was already amazing.

With two decades of trying new ideas, implementing creative thoughts and deeply massaging methods of making money – all with one common theme – this book will change your life and the lives of all who read it! Gerry was relentless in his pursuit of perfecting his ingenious ideas.

In 2009, I was honoured to be a guest at Gerry's initial seminar entitled Publish a Book & Grow Rich. Gerry had taken his decades of experience and put it into a seminar that would teach anyone how to write a book and use it for their personal and business benefit.

As is the usual with Gerry, the idea never stood still. It was constantly evolving, growing and benefitting anyone who would follow the easy steps to making their personal dreams of becoming an author come true.

I have authored 10 books since 1994. One was published using a traditional publisher and the others were all self-published. Meeting Gerry in 1991 and seeing how a book impacted the audience inspired me to write my first book. It changed my life.

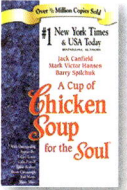 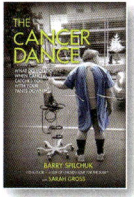  
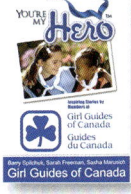   

Barry Spilchuk

Being connected with Gerry for more than 25 years has brought me so many blessings: Marketing smarts, sharing the stage, uplifting so many souls together, experiencing his overwhelming generosity – firsthand – and most importantly, friendship. It's a huge blessing when you have a friend who will tell you the truth – even if the truth isn't popular.

What you are about to experience by reading – and more importantly, DOING – this book is nothing less than a transformation of self. You are invited to implement each step of this book to embrace your dream of becoming an author. It may be scary – good! What worthwhile endeavour isn't? I promise you it will be worth it.

You can smash through any fears and terror barriers by consistently taking one more step towards your dream every day and constantly holding the vision of becoming a published author in your mind.

Soon, you will hold your book in your hand and then your journey towards cementing your personal legacy will continue.

Think of all the good!

Barry Spilchuk,
Co-author, *A Cup of Chicken Soup for the Soul*
Founder, www.TheLEGACY.club

These Black Card Books authors attended my Publish a Book & Grow Rich bootcamp:

GET YOUR FREE* TICKET HERE

www.publishabookandgrowrich.com/freeticket

*Not applicable in every country.

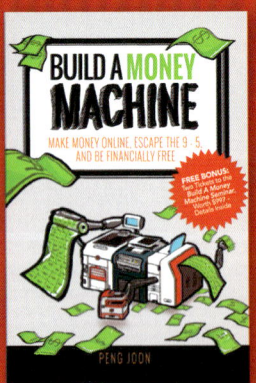

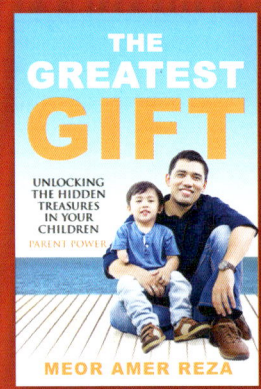

Contents

INTRODUCTION — 1

Yeah, publishing a book sounds cool, but what the heck should I write about so that I can make so much money my back hurts taking all of that money to the bank?

Chapter 1: PLAN IT — 19

Get the Right Book to Maximize the Effect on Your Bottom Line.

- What to Write About?

- The Critical 3 – The Formula That Will Show You Exactly What to Write About.

- Primary Objective (P.O.)

- Target Population (T.POP.)

- Needs/Desires/Problems (N.D.P.)

Chapter 2: **WRITE IT**   35

How to Write a Book in 40 Hours – Yes, It's Possible!

- The WRITE IT System™ is a proprietary system that will allow you to blueprint your book and allow you to write your entire book by answering questions and writing in five-minute chunks. Anyone can write for five minutes.

Chapter 3: **PUBLISH IT**   63

All the Boring Technical Stuff about How to Get a Book That Will Rock Your World.

- Write a Killer Title.

- Covers That Stop People in Their Tracks and Compel Them to Read Your Book.

- The Ins and Outs of Production… Become a Publishing Expert in 40 Minutes *(which is about how long it will take you to read this part)*.

- How I Got Major Celebrity Endorsements/ Forewords, and How You Can Too – It's Easy with My Secret Trick.

Chapter 4: **FUND IT** 103

Only Read This Chapter If You Want to Make Money Flow Directly to You Even before You Write a Single Word of Your Book.

- The Cash Concept.

- The Gerry Robert FUND IT™ System.

- Sell Books Using a Simple Little Buy Now Card™.

- See The System That Has Generated Millions of Dollars by Selling Ads in the Back of Books.

- One Tool (Feature Profile) That Will Bring in an Additional $6,000 to $10,000.

- How to Sell a BONUS Chapter for $7,500 to $10,000 to a JV Partner.

- Generate More Than $3,000 per Speech Using the FUND IT™ Speaking System.

- The Magic Formula That Helped Ann Lim Earn $5,100 in a 15-Minute Talk *(The Order Form Close)*.

Chapter 5: MOVE IT 137

What to Do with Your Book That Will Bring in More Prospects than You Know What to Do with and Cause the CASH to FLOW in Your Direction.

- Why Your Marketing Sucks and How a Book Can Make You a National Hero.

- The Campaigns That Work EVERY TIME for EVERYONE to Sell Books by the Truckload.

- MOVE IT – What to Do with Your Book That Will Bring in More Prospects than You Know What to Do with.

CONCLUSION 195

The Most Important Part of This Entire Book.

BONUS CHAPTER 197

RESOURCES THE AUTHOR RECOMMENDS 207

TESTIMONIALS 225

You CAN Do This!!!

Introduction

Yeah, publishing a book sounds cool but what the heck should I write about so that I can make so much money my back hurts taking all of that money to the bank?

In my mid-20s, I met a financial mentor. I met him through my friend Mark Victor Hansen, of the *Chicken Soup for the Soul* fame. Mark saw me on TV. I believe it was on Dr. Robert Schuller's show called *The Hour of Power* from the Crystal Cathedral. Mark saw my appearance and got in touch with me, and we became fast friends.

He told me that he could introduce me to his mentor who had helped him make a lot of money. I went to this person's seminar. There were 800 people at the event but I was the only one who gave him a copy of my book when I was introduced to him. Of course, when I autographed my book, I also wrote down my telephone number. I was shocked when he called me the next day and suggested we get together for coffee. See *how the power of a book can help you stand out in a crowd?*

In the first conversation I had with him, he asked me one question and made two statements that put me on a whole new course of life.

His first question was, "How much is the most amount of money you've ever made in this single year?"

Well, I told him boastfully that I had earned $100,000 the year before. I thought it was pretty good; no one in my family had made that much; none of my friends either.

Then he made the first of two life-altering statements: *"That's garbage!"*

What? He told me that $100,000 a year was garbage, that I should be earning that in a month. A month!

I almost flipped! I had never even considered such a huge amount. It was way, way, way beyond what I thought I could ever earn. Heck, I was working like a dog to earn the $100,000 in a year, and now he was telling me I could do this in a month – come on!

I don't know what you'd say if someone told you that you could make in a month what you are making in a whole year, but I didn't say to him, "Okay, great guru, just tell me what to do and I'll do it." No, I took a much bolder approach: I started to fight with him.

Isn't it funny that whenever someone shares an idea with you that's outside of your paradigm or your belief system, you tend to reject or ridicule the idea, even if you would really like the idea?

I started to fight with him. So I gave him every reason in the world as to why I could never make that much in a month. I told him, "I don't have any money."

Entrepreneurs know all too well that just because you are bringing in $100,000 doesn't mean you take home that much. That's what was happening to me. I was earning $100,000 but it was costing me $125,000 to get it.

I continued arguing: "I'm young. I'm only 25 years old. Besides you don't know my story. Look, I grew up in poverty; my family was supported by the State. My parents could not even provide the basics like a home and food without the government's help."

I told him that I didn't feel particularly smart. I got kicked out of school when I was 15.

So I kept telling him all these reasons why I could NEVER make in a month what I was making annually.

Then he drops the second statement. It was worse than the first... He looked at me square in the eyes and said, "You are a jerk!"

He called me a jerk! And let's face it, if somebody calls your income *garbage* and you a *jerk* in the first five minutes of meeting, it's either going to be a pretty brief meeting or maybe you should shut up and listen to what the guy has to say.

And I thought to myself, what if he's right? What if it is possible, to make every month what I'm making now in a year? I thought to myself, "What if I could just do it for one month!" Just once.

Would you like something like that to happen to you? Then don't reject new ideas. I promise you that this book will present ideas to you that are outside of your 'box', your mental programming and even outside of your comfort zone. Just keep an open mind. What you are about to read has completely changed my life and the lives of thousands of people. It can happen to you too!

I just decided to shut up and do everything he told me. I wanted to separate myself from the masses of people who go to seminars and don't do anything with the information afterwards. If he told me to write something, I would write it. If he told me to put my hand up, I'd put my hand up. If he told me to read a chapter of a book, I'd read it 30 times.

I just did what he said. And 12 months later, I was making $100,000 or more per month. My income shot to $1,000,000. It was incredible. Now, I routinely generate $1,000,000 in a single weekend. I've used the material you will read about here to generate more than $200,000,000 into my (and my business partners') bank accounts. This works!

In *Think and Grow Rich*, Napoleon Hill said the money's going to start coming, and when it does, it will come so fast and so furiously, you'll be wondering where it has been in all of the lean years.

So if you argue that this could never happen to you, you keep that. If you argue that you could never make that kind of money, you keep that.

If you argue that it's not as easy as this guy is telling me, you keep that.

You have to watch what you say and watch what you argue for.

YOU CAN DO THIS!

What You Argue for – You Get to Keep

You don't need money!

You don't need education!

You don't need a degree!

You don't need a fancy job!

You don't even need a fancy idea!

You don't need an exceptional skill!

You don't even have to know much about your topic.

You don't need to be an expert. You can interview the experts and their credibility will accrue to you. More on this later.

This Is Not a Conventional Publishing Book

- Don't try to find a publisher!
- Don't sell books in bookstores.
- Sell books before you have written a single word.
- Don't bother with book reviewers.
- Give your books away for FREE.
- Don't join a writers' group or club.
- There is no such thing as 'writer's block'.
- Don't worry about spelling.
- Grammar is overrated.
- Stop wasting time trying to get "BESTSELLER" status – it means virtually nothing!

What I'm recommending is that you publish your book yourself. Self-publishing is a very acceptable form of publishing and, in my opinion, the far more lucrative way to go.

After the creation of desktop-publishing tools in the mid-1980s, there was a flood of self-published books. In those days, 'self-published' meant that you couldn't find a real publisher because your book was crappy. The stigma and suspect nature of self-publishing now are far less than in those days, but they still exist.

Seth Godin, the prolific author and speaker, recently announced that he's going the self-publishing route. So did Guy Kawasaki.

I am suggesting that you form your own publishing company; name it something other than your own name. Gerry Robert Books doesn't sound as credible as Prime Books.

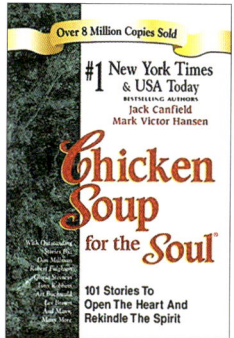

You should stop trying to find a traditional publisher. Why would I say that? Because of the issue of probabilities and of profit. The chance of you being accepted by a traditional publisher is so small that it's not worth the effort. For every book that is accepted by traditional publishers, they may reject 3,000 to 5,000 manuscripts. I don't like those odds.

But you say, Jack Canfield and Mark Victor Hansen have done okay through a traditional publisher. Sure they did. Jack and Mark are friends of mine and I've known them since well before the *Chicken Soup* days. Seriously though, what do you think the chances are that you (or I) will sell 500 million books? It could happen but let's be realistic here.

The main reason to self-publish is the profit motive. In this book, I will teach you numerous ways to generate a significant amount of money using your book. So what I'm talking about is ENTREPRENEURIAL publishing. You could never use most of the money-making strategies that I describe in this book if you go the traditional route.

In this book, I will show you how my students routinely generate tens of thousands of dollars before they write a single word. I will show you how to generate

Guy Kawasaki

Seth Godin

leads within a few weeks of putting my plan in place. You will see exactly how to use your book to further your own objectives – something traditional publishers have no interest in.

One thing most people do not understand is the timing in traditional publishing. If you are lucky enough to be picked to be published, you won't see your book in print for 16 to 18 months after submission. You will learn in this book how to see tangible results from your book in 16 to 18 days, not months.

Most published author friends of mine are shocked about how little their publishers do to market books. Many of these publishers are in dire straits. They live and die on the few books that become bestsellers – the *50 Shades* books or the *Chicken Soup for the Soul* books. In fact, it's said that the original *Chicken Soup* publisher, Health Communications Inc., was about to declare bankruptcy before meeting with Jack Canfield and Mark Victor Hansen.

Selling books in bookstores is a dumb waste of time for most of you. Unless your book takes off and becomes the next *Rich Dad Poor Dad* (and the odds of that are a million to one), there are many more profitable ways to make money with your book. Despite all the books that

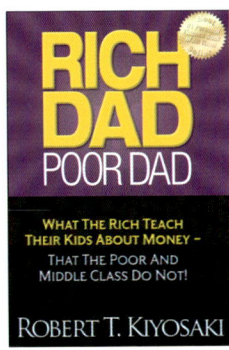

say the opposite, selling books in bookstores is tough and unless your book sells thousands of copies in the first two months, it'll be yanked off the shelves to make room for the 5,000 other books coming down the pike. They take forever to pay you and they keep 60% to 80% of the profit. Stupid!

Traditional publishers are great at MAKING books but terrible when it comes to SELLING books.

"Traditional publishers stop marketing a book when the month-long introduction ends or it stops selling – whichever comes first."

— Guy Kawasaki and Shawn Welch, authors of *APE: Author, Publisher, Entrepreneur – How to Publish a Book*

"Publishers don't use marketing to cause books to sell well – they help books that are already selling well to sell even better."

— Guy Kawasaki and Shawn Welch, authors of *APE: Author, Publisher, Entrepreneur – How to Publish a Book*

Idiotic authors, who rarely have made big money in this game, make recommendations in their 'How to become an author' books, regurgitating nonsense about how to sell in bookstores. They will tell you about social media (waste of time), they will spew about gimmick marketing tricks (manipulating bestseller lists), they will wax eloquent about stupid things like contests, book signings, buying advertising. If the author of these publishing books has not earned more than $1,000,000 in a single year from books, don't read their drivel, and I can tell you most are just that! DRIVEL.

Another thing to consider is that when you use the traditional publishing methods, you lose all control of your book. They decide the design of the cover. They often even pick the title. That is ridiculous in my way of thinking. How can some chump working at the head office, making a tiny salary, know about you, your plans, your market and your aspirations?

I think what you should do is go do it alone. Of course, you get educated, learn the best practices from those of us who bring in millions every single year with our books, but do it my way.

Look, the real money in this is not trying to make $10 to $20 selling a book – it's all the other sources of income that give you the big payday.

AUTHORS WANTED

**Publish with Black Card Books –
The Entrepreneurial Publisher**

One alternative is to partner your book with me.
I've generated over $200,000,000 in the publishing world
and I have a totally unique model.
I've turned the publishing world upside-down.
If you want to know how I do it, just scan the code or go to
www.publishabookandgrowrich.com/authorswanted

> "Someone once asked me how much I made from my first book. The answer I gave was $10 million. The book itself only paid me $35,000 in royalties, but the speaking engagements, spin-off books, newsletters, columns, bootcamps, consulting, and wide open doors resulted in the remaining $9,965,000."
>
> — Jay Conrad Levinson, author of *Guerrilla Marketing*

Jay Conrad Levinson

Why try and make a few bucks selling books, which is a lot harder than you think, when you could make thousands selling your products or services?

When I went from poverty to earning millions in a single year, I wasn't doing what everyone else does. I did what wealthy people do. When it comes to book publishing, it's not about selling books; it's about using a book as a center pin to multiple sources of income.

In the "FUND IT" chapter, you will see how our students raise all the money they need to cover the printing, editing, designing, etc., from other people. In many cases, they actually make a profit before the book goes to press.

What I'm talking about here is a physical book, not an eBook. eBooks are a dime a dozen. You can never get publicity, be perceived as an expert, sell speaking engagements, attract leads and open doors with a stupid little eBook. You need a real book.

> "Few authors actually make money from the sales of their books."
> — Rick Frishman and Robyn Freedman Spizman, authors of *101 Bestselling Book Publicity: The Insider's Guide to Promoting Your Book – and Yourself*

Everyone knows that you can type a few thousand words, run a spell check, PDF the 'book' and presto, you're an author. That isn't even in the same realm as publishing a 200-page softcover book.

Are you aware that you can print a book for less than $1 or $2? That's right. If you purchase 2,000 copies, you can end up with $30,000 to $40,000 worth of retail value. This is partly why my system works so well. I suggest giving books away. Why wouldn't you do that? Can you find a cheaper, more powerful way to attract leads? The perceived cost of a 100-page softcover book is close to $20-$30, but it costs less than $2 to produce. You do the math!

> "A book isn't written... It is engineered!"
> — Gerry Robert

Why Haven't You Already Published Your Book?

I ask this question all over the world in my seminars. I get many excuses, (ahem) reasons! They range from not knowing what to write about, not feeling worthy, not feeling like an expert, thinking that there are already too many books on the subject and the list goes on. The real reason, in my research, is that people suffer from what I call THE LITERARY GENIUS COMPLEX.

They feel like their book must be…

- World-changing.
- Earth-shattering.
- Industry-revolutionizing.
- Personality-altering.
- History-making.
- An incomprehensibly complicated work of art.
- Totally original.
- With never-before-heard-of content.
- Massively-sized.
- Masterfully-written.
- In perfect English.
- A one-of-a-kind book.
- Without one single spelling mistake!

You need to let go of the notion that your book has to be perfect. You have what it takes right now to write a book. If not, I'll show you later how to research from those who are the experts and, by association, build up your credibility.

Why a Book?

When you become an author, you instantly gain several advantages to help you promote yourself and can earn more money or accomplish whatever you want your book to do for you.

I'm not talking about 'bestseller' or being the next Malcolm Gladwell or John Grisham. I'm talking about becoming an author to accomplish a very specific goal… your Primary Objective.

AUTHORity

A Book Gives You Credibility

People who write books are perceived as experts. Prospects see your name and face on a book cover, and in our culture, you are viewed as credible and as an authority figure.

Plain and simple, the more credible you are, the more sales you will make. Why? Because people will trust you more.

A Book Gives You FREE Advertising

Despite popular opinion to the opposite, radio stations, TV shows, magazines and newspapers are looking to give you FREE publicity. They start every day with an empty page and they want to give you exposure.

The value of this seems obvious but when you are visible and people see you on TV or hear you on the radio, it helps your business. A book has given me over $10 million of FREE advertising.

Black Card Books author Meor Amer Reza has been featured on local and national radio and TV because of his book. He uses the book to gain publicity for his speaking and his coaching program.

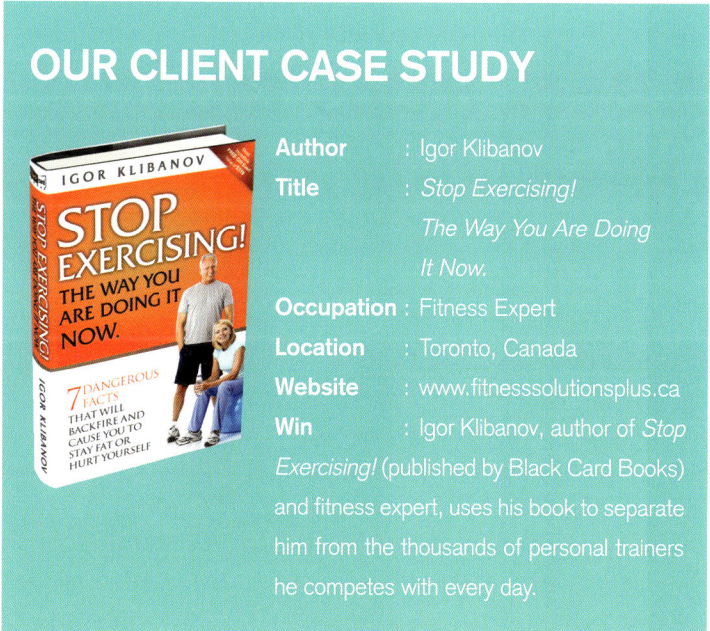

OUR CLIENT CASE STUDY

Author : Igor Klibanov
Title : *Stop Exercising! The Way You Are Doing It Now.*
Occupation : Fitness Expert
Location : Toronto, Canada
Website : www.fitnesssolutionsplus.ca
Win : Igor Klibanov, author of *Stop Exercising!* (published by Black Card Books) and fitness expert, uses his book to separate him from the thousands of personal trainers he competes with every day.

12 | INTRODUCTION

A Book Helps You Differentiate Yourself

There may be thousands of people who offer what you offer. Why should they buy from you? Competition is stiff today!

Imagine this: A real estate agent is making a presentation to the owners of a nice house worth more than $2 million. Of course, they will likely interview several agents before granting the listing to one of them. Before leaving, our imaginary agent says something like this: "Mr. Jones, I know and fully expect you will speak with several agents before making this important decision. Can I ask you to do just one thing before making that decision? Please read a chapter in my book." Then she autographs a copy of her book for the homeowner.

Which has more impact for a real estate agent?

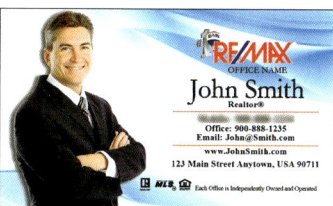

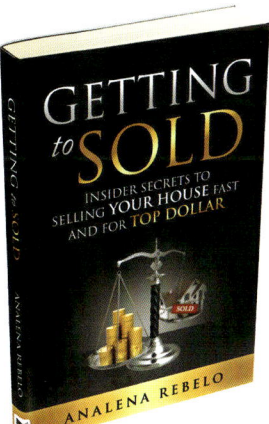

What has just happened to her competition? Obliterated!

Black Card Books author Analena Rebelo separates herself from the 40,000+ agents in her city of Toronto!

A Book Is the Best Recruiting Tool for Network Marketing

In 2005, I did a test to see if we could use a book to recruit people to a network marketing company I had signed up with: Nikken.

In my first month in the business, I broke every record in the company for personal sales using my book as the principle tool to recruit distributors. They sent me a cheque for $17,359.41.

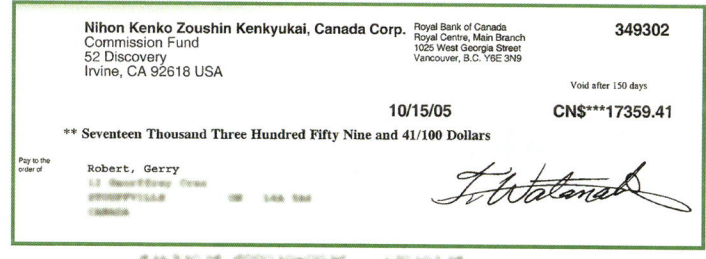

You will never convince me that a book won't work in Network Marketing. I'm no longer involved with any company but I do endorse the industry (with a few caveats!).

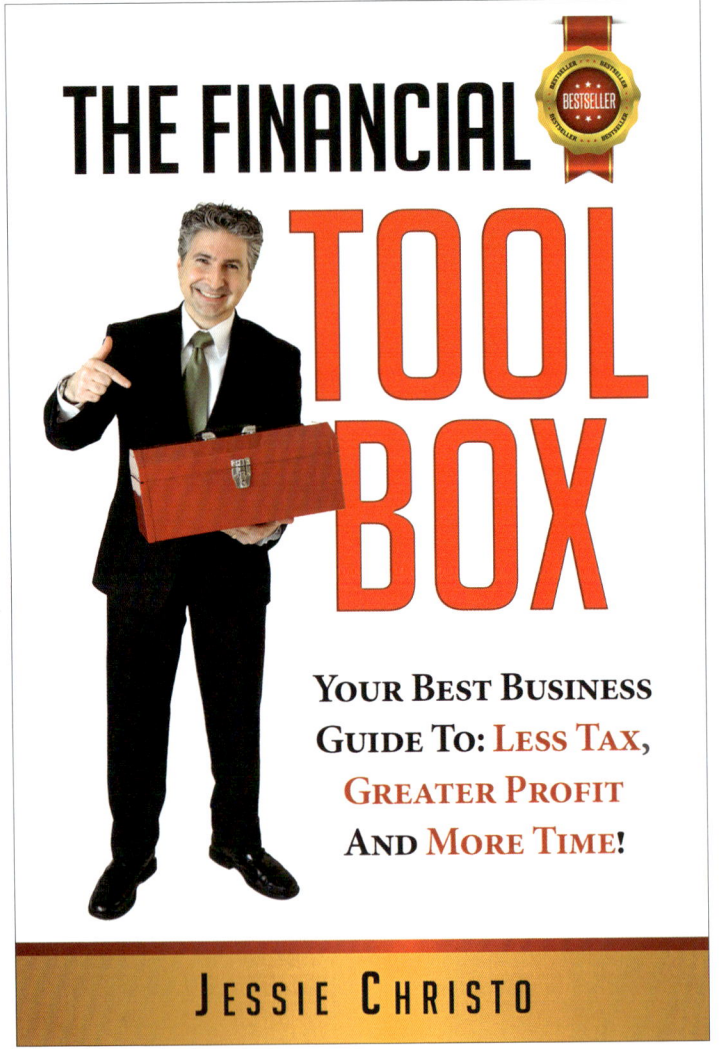

A Book Helps You Get Referrals

One financial advisor we published is Jessie Christo. He offers his book *The Financial Toolbox* to his existing clients. He tells them to give a FREE copy of this book to their friends. In the book itself, which he autographs in advance, he offers a FREE first visit for friends of existing customers. He's busier than ever before.

Download a FREE copy of this book!

A Book Helps You Recruit

Dave Ogunnaike, author of *The Millionaire Genius* (published by Black Card Books), uses his book to build instant rapport for his direct-sales organization. He needs to recruit thousands of agents and his book pre-sells him to prospects and gets the whole sales force motivated to introduce him to their friends and prospects.

A Book Opens Doors

Black Card Books author Sindi Zilwa wanted to meet CEOs of large enterprises to offer her unique auditing services.

She wrote *The ACE Model – Winning Formula For Audit Committees.* Now, before making a sales call to the CEO, she sends them an autographed copy of this book along with the following…

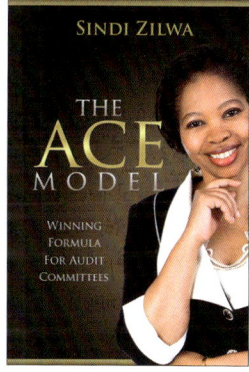

Dear Mr. CEO,

My mentor told me that I should give my book to the hundred most positive people in this city. I hear you're one of them. Enjoy the book!

*Yours truly,
Sindi Zilwa*

A Book Attracts Prospects

Instead of cold calling or any other outdated rejection-based strategy, why not make the people who are likely to buy your product or service come directly to you?

How? Do what educational consultant Rozieta Shaary did. Prior to publishing *Happy Kids* with us, she would advertise her practice with an ad that cost $1,500. She would typically receive 15 to 20 calls every time that ad ran. She thought she could do better.

After attending our seminar, I showed her how to write a book and offer it for FREE in that ad. The result? She consistently gets 300 to 500 phone calls every three days from the same $1,500 ad.

Shaary uses her book to boost advertising response.

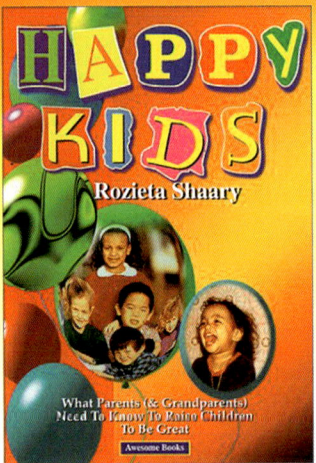

A Book Can Even Get You a Better Job

How many résumés are submitted along with a copy of the person's book? Do you think that would separate you from every other applicant? It sure would. That's what happened to my client Han Kok Kwang. He wanted to change management consulting firms and used a book to get himself a better job, with a higher pay and in a more senior position.

A Book Can Help You Change Your Target Market

I published Colorado Optometrist Dr. Lou Spinozzi's book, *What Your Bright Child Can't See*. He had a desire to work more with children. He had developed a new procedure to diagnose learning challenges in children. He was passionate about that. So he asked me how he could use a book to reach more children. I suggested this title. Our art department came up with this powerful cover and now Dr. Spinozzi spends most of his time working with children.

A Book Can Get You Speaking Engagements

Accountant Davidde Ong uses his book to get speaking engagements. The content of the book is simply a compilation of anonymous jokes that circulate via the Internet. He simply reads the jokes at his speaking engagements.

A Book Gives Your Marketing Long-Term Shelf Life

One day, I got a speaking engagement to address the annual conference of Mister Transmission, a Canadian franchise. I asked the president who booked me how he picked me. He explained that in 1986, he heard me speak at a Scarborough Chamber of Commerce breakfast meeting and was surprised that I gave everyone there a FREE copy of my first book, *Conquering Life's Obstacles*. No speaker had ever given a book away for FREE to an entire audience before – that stood out to him even almost 15 years later. When he was looking for a speaker, he went to his bookshelf and my book stood out, and he wondered if I was still speaking. I was, and he booked me. How many of your fancy brochures would be on your prospects' bookshelves 15 years after you gave it to them? They paid me $5,000 for a one-hour talk. I did have to wait 15 years, but giving away books in 1986 paid off big time; it was a very worthwhile investment indeed!

NO ONE EVER THROWS OUT A BOOK.

FREE* TICKET

Attend the Publish A Book & Grow Rich bootcamp.

PLAN IT | WRITE IT | PUBLISH IT | FUND IT | MOVE IT

Scan the QR code or go to
www.publishabookandgrowrich.com/freeticket
*Not applicable in every country.

Chapter One

PLAN IT
WRITE IT
PUBLISH IT
FUND IT
MOVE IT

"The average number of copies that most books sell, according to street wisdom, is a few hundred."

— Guy Kawasaki and Shawn Welch, authors of *APE: Author, Publisher, Entrepreneur – How to Publish a Book*

1

PLAN IT

Get the Right Book to Maximize the Effect on Your Bottom Line.

- What to Write About?
- The Critical 3 – the Formula That Will Show You Exactly What to Write About.
- Primary Objective (P.O.)
- Target Population (T.POP.)
- Needs/Desires/Problems (N.D.P.)

Get a book...
But get the RIGHT one!

Let's Talk Money

How long have you been *thinking* about writing a book? When you figure out your MAGIC NUMBER, a basic calculation to determine the 24-month value of each new customer you sell, you will become very depressed. A book is a financial asset but it'll do no one any good while it sits dormant inside your head.

Calculate Your Magic Number

You need to find out the financial value of each new customer. This is a very basic calculation based on two years. You want to calculate your MAGIC NUMBER using the following formulas:

> **I have been thinking about writing a book for _____ years.**

A Per New Client

On average or ideally, how much do you earn from each new sale over a two-year period? If you sell to someone, how much do you make? If there is a wide range in that amount, average it out or calculate how much you would make from an *ideal* client. If you are new to an industry or you haven't yet set up a business around your book, then either ask people who are more familiar with your chosen industry or project what you would make from ideal clients.

B Number of Referrals

On average or ideally, how many referrals would you receive from a new client (over two years)? Keep in mind that, as an author, your credibility, your believability and your status go way up, making you much easier to refer.

C Total Referral Income

Multiply (A) by (B) to determine your Total Referral Income. Let's say you earn $1,000 from a new client (A) and they get you two Referrals (B), then your Referral Income would be $2,000 because you make $1,000 per new client.

A Per New Client

C Total Referral Income

D Your Magic #

Now, add (A) + (C) to calculate your Magic Number. That is how much each new customer brings you – potentially!

Just ask yourself how many new customers you could get if you printed 2,000 copies of your book and used it as a marketing tool or a lead generator and literally just gave them away to prospects. Seriously, this should depress some of you. If you think about how many years you have been procrastinating on this, you will cringe at how much money you have left on the table.

B Number of Referrals

D Your Magic #

The Fastest Path to the Biggest Cash!

Before I get into which is the best book for you to publish first, let me share with you the difference between a PASSION book and a PROFIT book.

Passion Book vs. Profit Book

You might be passionate about a book topic or genre (poetry or biography) but there might not be any money in that topic or that genre. For example, there is little money in novels (typically) or children's books. I'm wanting to get you to think 'Empire' here. You want to think about the money in and around your book. The big money is not in the book – it's in selling your products or services; or selling speaking engagements, or seminar tickets; or coaching or consulting services.

> "All writers think of what they do as an art. Smart writers understand that writing is also a business. Really smart writers see themselves also as entrepreneurs."
>
> — Barry Eisler, author of *Be the Monkey: A Conversation About the New World of Publishing*

Because of that, I recommend your first book be related to an existing business if at all possible. If you are a real estate agent, do a book on real estate, not on alcoholism. You can make money next week with real estate, assuming you are not looking to leave that industry. If you do a book on alcoholism, it will take you months to create a business plan, raise funds, design an offer or service renderings, design marketing materials, etc. I want you to make money in the next six weeks... that's pretty hard if you have to set up a new business.

So in this example, the alcohol book would be considered a passion book, but the real estate book I would classify as the profit book and that's the one I would suggest you do first. You can always do the passion one later, once you've put a few hundred thousand dollars in your bank account.

The Critical 3 Formula

1. The P.O. Primary Objective	What do I want my book to do for me?
2. The T.POP. Target Population	Who am I going after?
3. The N.D.P. Needs, Desires, Problems	What keeps the T.POP. up at night?

1. Determine Your P.O. (Primary Objective)

The first step, before you write a single word, is to think about what you want the book to do for YOU. Most people have ever only thought about what the book will do for the reader. I say, that is unimportant at this stage. Figure out what you want the book to do for you and let that dictate what you will write about.

Let me illustrate this by telling you something that happened to me in Los Angeles several years ago: I had given a lecture on book publishing when someone approached me at the end of my talk and asked me to have a look at their manuscript; this happens a lot when people find out I own one of the fastest-growing book publishing companies in the world based upon titles acquired. It was a book of poems. Poems! He could see the less than enthusiastic reaction on my face. He pointed his finger in my face and said, "Hold it, these are not normal poems. They are designed to teach men how to connect more intimately with their male children." I have three boys and this seemed like a different idea.

"Wow!" I said, "Let me have a look." I read one of the poems and loved it. It made me cry a little; it was so good. So, is that a good book? Sure.

My first question is always: *What do you want this book to do for you?* He answered quickly; he had thought about this before. "I want this book to get me publicity, because if I get on radio or TV, I'll invite men to my seminars, and if they come to my seminars, I will change the life of these men and of their boys."

Again... "Wow..." What a great objective.

The problem is that he'll never achieve that objective with that book. You'll never hear a radio talk-show host say, "Hey, when we come back from the break, we are going to have a guy who wrote a poetry book on next!" That will never happen. "If publicity is what you want," I told him, "don't write a book of poems; write a book entitled *How to Make Sure Your Boys Don't End Up Like Michael Jackson!* – that will get publicity."

So determine your P.O. (Primary Objective) first. Ask yourself, if your book could only do one thing for YOU, what would you want that to be?

Possible Primary Objectives

Build a database

Book appointments

Generate traffic in my establishment

Sell seminar tickets

Sell books

Speak for a fee

Build credibility

Meet people

Open doors

Improve advertising results

Do TV interviews

Become an expert

Get better clients

Sell products or services

Make money from book sales

Tell your story

Get a job

Get a better job

Create multiple sources of income

Create more FREE time

Travel

Become a speaker

Create awareness

Influence your industry

Get a position in an association

Get a consulting contract

Speak at conventions

Educate people

Impact others

Be taken more seriously

Change lives

Open new markets

Open a new niche market

Become more visible

Write newspaper columns

Build my brand

Meet famous people

Position myself as an authority

Get More Business

OUR CLIENT CASE STUDY

Author : Ahmad-Shah Duranai
Title : *The Leadership Zone*
Occupation : Consultant
Location : Toronto, Canada
Website : www.theleadershipzone31.com
Win : Ahmad says that his book, published by Black Card Books, is the single best business tool he's ever used to open doors. He's been able to use his book to get appointments with CEOs of banks – appointments that were previously completely out of his reach.

My Primary Objective:

Do TV Interviews (ELLEN)

Get Publicity to Promote Your Brand

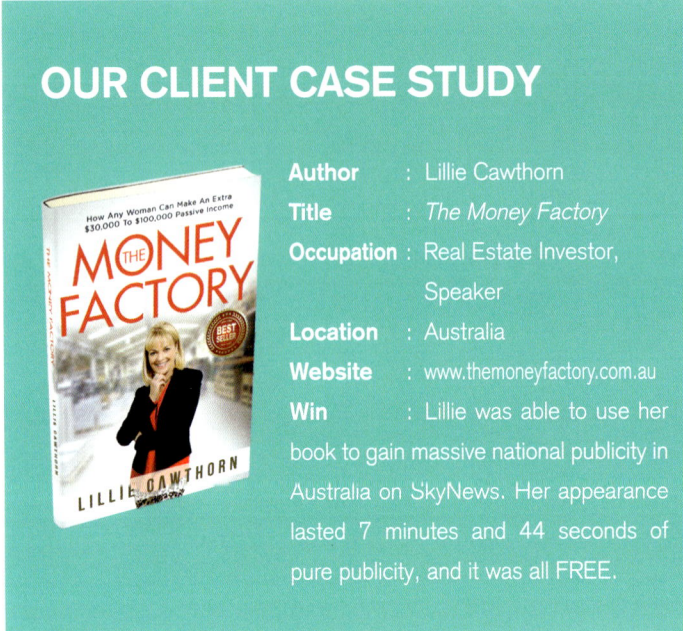

OUR CLIENT CASE STUDY

Author	: Lillie Cawthorn
Title	: *The Money Factory*
Occupation	: Real Estate Investor, Speaker
Location	: Australia
Website	: www.themoneyfactory.com.au
Win	: Lillie was able to use her book to gain massive national publicity in Australia on SkyNews. Her appearance lasted 7 minutes and 44 seconds of pure publicity, and it was all FREE.

"The best way to become acquainted with a subject is to write a book about it."

— Benjamin Disraeli

2. Analyze Your T.POP. (Target Population)

The next thing you must analyze is your reader. Not from a psychographic point of view (we will do that next) but from a demographic point of view. Who are these people? And don't say EVERYONE. You can't market to everyone. Get specific about who your book will be geared towards. Below is a list of some of the categories that will help you isolate the best buyers for your products or services.

Age	% Singles	Where do they like to eat?
Sex	% Students	Where do they shop?
% Male	Any trauma	How much do they spend on…?
% Female	Medical history	What makes them mad?
Occupation	Income	What political party?
Level	Net worth	What do they do for fun?
Children	Education	What makes them buy?
% Married	% College	How many of them are there?
% Divorced	% High school	Where do they live?
		In the city?
		Rural?
		How many friends do they have?
		What organizations do they belong to?
		Do they take vacations?

Other Questions to Help You Determine Your T.POP.:

- What things do they do in their spare time?
- What is their demographics?
- Where do they congregate?
- If so, what do they talk about?
- Are they on social media sites?
- If so, which ones mainly?
- What are they doing at this stage in their lives?
- What other books have they bought?
- If you asked them why they would buy your book, what would they say to you?

My T.POP.:

_____

3. Analyze the N.D.P. (Needs, Desires, Problems) of Your T.POP.

"'How will I benefit from writing a book?' Their answers to this other question include: 'It's good for my visibility.' 'To make money.' 'It will help me get speaking gigs and consulting engagements.' 'It's good for my company.' 'It will make me a thought leader.' Any of these reasons may be true for the author, but they are not relevant for readers. Think about this: How often do you peruse Barnes & Noble or Amazon while wondering how you can help an author achieve his or her personal goals?"

— Guy Kawasaki and Shawn Welch, authors of *APE: Author, Publisher, Entrepreneur – How to Publish a Book*

What you must do is find out what keeps your target market up at night. The more you understand their pain and problems, the better your book can provide solid solutions for them. The more you understand this, the better this will go for you. This is probably one of the most valuable things I will share in this entire book.

Zig Ziglar said, *"If you give enough people what THEY WANT, they will give you what you want."* People today are overwhelmed with stress, debt, disease and marketing messages. They have so many things that cause them pain. The subject of your book should provide answers to these very problems. If you're not sure what to write about, ask yourself what their biggest problems are and write about that. Period.

What follows is a list of potential problems or desires your T.POP. might have. You know them much better than anyone so add to the list, but get to the bottom of their Needs, Desires and Problems.

Stress related	Feels not being heard
Self-esteem related	No time
Vocational	Boss pressures
Relational	Speed issues
Financial	Fear
Feels confined	Economic
Family related	Is tired
Future related	Tired of conflicts
Negativity of industry	Lack of sex
Wants more time	Wants to stop struggling
Desire to succeed	Got bad advice
Needs customers	Needs to start over
Confused	Economic uncertainty
Unsure about changes	Distrustful
Feels stuck	Angry
Tired of rat race	Hates the government
Feels like a failure	Skeptical
Wants to make a difference	

My T.POP.'s #1 N.D.P.:

_____

No matter what you are looking to do with your book, you need to analyze who will respond to your message. If you are looking to make a lot of money selling your book, then you must choose a subject that will sell. If you want publicity, you might want to consider controversy. If it's to establish you as an expert, the cover takes priority.

Knowing exactly who you are going after will make a huge difference.

Look at it this way: First, you figure out what you want the book to do for YOU – Primary Objective. Then, you figure out who will give that to you – T.POP. Lastly, you determine what keeps them up at night because if you can solve that (N.D.P. - Needs/Desires/Problems), they will give you your P.O.

By the way, the N.D.P. also becomes the basis of your book speech, seminar and/or coaching services.

The Photocopier Salesperson

Imagine a hardworking photocopier salesperson wanting to get ahead. Let's say they bought this book or attended my Publish a Book & Grow Rich bootcamp and got excited about using a book to improve their sales.

The temptation for this person would be to write a book related to photocopiers. They might include chapters on how to buy the right machine or how many pages it might print in a minute or what to look for in a service contract – all of which is of little interest to readers. People today can smell a rat from a mile away. A book can be the best brochure on the planet if you do it right. The key is that it can be a brochure, but it must not look like one.

Let's face it: A book on photocopiers by a photocopier salesperson smells fishy. Instead, what if this person followed my system? What if they first established what they wanted the book to do for them (Determine your P.O. – Primary Objective)? It's conceivable that the main thing they would like to have the book do for them is open doors. Let's face it, it's tough selling photocopiers these days. With the P.O. established, the system calls for an analysis of the T.POP. (Target Population).

Who buys photocopiers? If this salesperson spent a few minutes thinking about their *ideal* prospect, they might find that the best prospects were office managers between the ages of 45 and 60. This person typically worked at the company for 10 years or more. They earned between $37,000 and $52,000 per year. So now, having established what the book would do for them (Open Doors) and who the ideal reader is (Office Managers), the only thing left to work out is what their Needs, Desires and Problems (N.D.P.) are. That is, what keeps this person up at night? What concerns do they have in life? What do they worry about the most?

In our workshops, I often ask the audience what keeps an office manager up at night. The responses usually include things like:

- How to save money when buying a photocopier.

- How reliable are these machines?

- How many pages per minute can it spit out?

- How much power does it use?

- What is the cost of a toner and how much will it use?

There's not an office manager on the planet who tosses and turns at night worrying about how many pages his stupid photocopier prints per minute. No siree. So it would be silly to write a book answering those issues. Instead, if they thought about it for a bit, they would discover that what keeps an office manager up at night might include:

- How can I get respect in the office?

- Why doesn't anyone acknowledge me in the office?

- What can I do to get my budgets approved?

- How can I get my boss to follow my recommendations?

Writing a book like this is so much better than *What You Need to Know Before You Buy a Photocopier*. This is too obviously written as a brochure to help sell photocopiers. Now imagine if this photocopier salesperson wrote a book called *How Office Managers Can Get the Respect They Deserve and Make Their Boss Do Just About Anything!*

Now the photocopier salesperson sends a copy of that book before he makes the sales call. How do you think that might change the welcome they would get from that prospect? How many books do you think the office manager got for FREE last week from an author? Where do you think this author might be invited to speak? Office Managers Association conventions! So be careful about the content of your book. For maximum effect, write a book that addresses those issues that are needs in the minds of your prospects.

By the way, don't worry if there are thousands of books written on your topic. We call that a clue! Since our methods don't typically involve competing with other books on the subject in bookstores, our strategies are much more powerful. For example, you can autograph a book with this inscription:

"My mentor told me to give my book to the 100 most positive people in this city… I hear you are one of them – Enjoy the book!"

In this scenario, do you think it would matter whatsoever that there might be tens of thousands of books written on your topic? Of course not. They would be very impressed by you and your book because it's about something that they struggle with – and besides, how many FREE books do you think they got last week?

Chapter Two

PLAN IT
WRITE IT
PUBLISH IT
FUND IT
MOVE IT

Get It DOWN,
Then Get It
RIGHT!

Let Go of Perfection.

Version ONE is better
than version NONE.

2

WRITE IT

How to Write a Book in 40 Hours – Yes, It's Possible!

- The WRITE IT System™ is a proprietary system that will allow you to blueprint your book and allow you to write your entire book by answering questions and writing in five-minute chunks. Anyone can write for five minutes.

The Write a Book in 40 Hours System

What if you never again had to struggle to write anything? What if I could show you a system that has worked for tens of thousands of people around the world? People just like you. What you are about to see is a way for you to get the book out of your head and onto paper. You cannot write a book in your head. The issue, though, is that it is precisely why you don't have your book in your hands yet. You don't have a track to run on or a way to pull that book out of your head. What follows will do exactly that for you.

Let Go of the Need to Be Perfect or Write the Biggest and Best Book Ever Written on Your Topic.

Write an 80-100 page book.

Excuses

I Don't Know What to Write About!

You don't have to write *Gone with the Wind*. Your book doesn't have to be the single best book on the topic ever written. All you need is a 100-page book. That's 10 chapters with about 10 pages in each chapter. Base your book on the N.D.P. (Needs/Desires/Problems) of your T.POP.

OUR CLIENT CASE STUDY

Author : Davidde Ong
Title : *Laugh Life*
Occupation : Accountant
Location : Singapore
Win : Davidde wanted to have a creative outlet for his sense of humour. He is an accountant and wanted to become an after-dinner humourous speaker. He didn't know what to write about. When I shared with him that he should let go of the enormous book idea he had originally, he came up with a very unique concept: He would share jokes that circulate around the Internet. That's all his book is – jokes – that others have written… he didn't even have to write it. You think you have to write *War and Peace?*

But There Are Too Many Books on My Topic!

So what? Who cares? Listen, if you use your book the way I am recommending here, it won't matter at all how many books there are on your topic. If you were to give a book to a prospect before you have your sales call with this person, do you think they will ever even think of the fact that there are thousands of books written on this topic? NO! How many books do you think they got last week for FREE? And signed by the author? NONE!

But I'm Not an Expert!

You don't have to be an expert to write a book. Who told you such nonsense? Do you think Napoleon Hill knew anything about wealth when he wrote *Think and Grow Rich*? NO! We are not using our books to kick Malcolm Gladwell off the bestseller list. We are using our books as marketing, branding and positioning tools. I tell people all the time, "Write the book, then you'll be qualified."

Who Will Read My Book?

Who cares about this? Most will probably not even read it at all. Just think of how many books you have on your bookshelf that you have not finished or even started. Your book has incredible marketing muscle whether they read it or not.

What Will Others Think of Me?

Who cares?

Be a Reporter

OUR CLIENT CASE STUDY

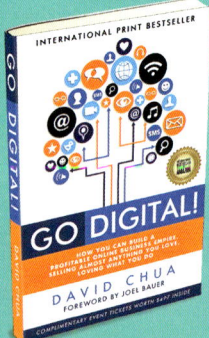

Author : David Chua
Title : *Go Digital!*
Occupation : Speaker and Coach
Location : Perth, Australia
Website : www.DavidChuaLive.com
Win : When I met David, he was a 20-something entrepreneur who had his eyes squarely on becoming a motivational speaker. I told him to write a book on wealth. He looked at me like I had two heads. How could such a young man write a book on wealth building? I told him to do exactly what Napoleon Hill did for *Think and Grow Rich:* Interview people who were wealthy.

By the way, David routinely gets publicity even though he's only in his twenties. I'll show you how to do exactly the same thing in our MOVE IT section.

There are many types of books:

- Here's my STORY.
- Here's my ADVICE.
- Here's my RESEARCH.

} If you're not an expert, interview them – be a reporter!

"If you interview 10 experts, you will be considered the 11th."

— Gerry Robert

Let's Get Started on Writing YOUR Book

Your Book Blueprint

If you decide to build a house, will you order a load of wood and just start nailing boards together, or would you draw a plan, a very specific plan, that covered every detail? We are about to create a very specific plan for your book – a blueprint.

The better your blueprint, the better your book – and the faster you will have it in print. This blueprint is designed, tested and proven to make it possible for you to get your first draft written within 40 hours. You will see how your left brain logical approach and your right brain creative resources are used in this blueprint and how they will assist you in writing your book and in being proud of the final product.

Stop thinking about it...

Let's get 'er DONE!

Get it DOWN, then get it RIGHT!

YOU CAN DO THIS!

Let's Go!

The Purpose

The purpose of this plan is to assist you in getting your book written. The first, largest and most intimidating step is to get your rough draft written.

Follow the format and you will have the major portion of your first draft written in 40 hours.

Just as it makes no sense to start out on a journey without a clear destination, a map and a plan on how to get there, it makes no sense to start on your book without a clear purpose, a map and a plan on how to get your book into print. Think of this guide as a map that will take you from where you are now to the day you will see your book:

What is your Mission Statement? *TRAIN YOUR MIND MUSCLE TO BE IN THE BEST SHAPE OF YOUR LIFE!*

Who are you writing this book for? *18+ to 100+*

What is the profile of your target reader? *18-70, Lacking Confidence & UNFIT*

What is the purpose of your book? *INSPIRE & CHANGE LIVES*

What is your end-in-mind in writing your book?

What would you like a reader to say as he or she reads your book?

What would you like a reader to do or to say after reading your book?

When would you like to have your book in print? *May 1st 2019*

You must have a very definite purpose for your book. How will you know that you have a very definite purpose? We covered that in an earlier session. Remember? The Primary Objective? You have it in writing and you can share it with someone you respect. How will you know that you do not have a very definite purpose? You do not have it down in writing.

Your Biggest Worry (It's Normal)

Forget your biggest worry: "I won't have enough to say. I don't know enough." When you sit down to actually write it, you will find that you have too much to say.

Your challenge will be to cut out material.

As entrepreneurs, we are always on the leading edge, we are always learning new things. What happens?

We forget how much we really know. The next time you're in a sales presentation, watch how carefully your prospect listens. Do you know what they're thinking?

"How does he or she know so much? Where do they learn all this stuff?"

They are saying to themselves, "I wish I knew what they know." Your very desire to write a book is proof that you have the ability to make it happen. Would you want to write a book about something of which you knew nothing about and had no interest? Decide right now that you are an informed writer. You know what you want to write; however, right now, you do not have your knowledge on paper.

Myths

- Writers are natural born writers.
- You have to write a million words to be an author.
- Good writers are driven by divine inspiration.
- Inspired writing is better than normal writing.
- If you just start writing, it will come.
- You have to wait until you're inspired.
- It must be perfect.
- Good writing is difficult.
- Good writing has something to do with good grammar.
- You have to be a Ph.D. or multimillionaire to author a book.
- Your experience isn't valid to be in a book.
- You must have achieved major accomplishments to write.

7 Steps to Write a Book in 40 Hours

Step 1: Write 15 Major Topics

Write down your chapter titles. These may change as you get into your book; however, this exercise will get the creative process moving… even if you're not creative.

If a good friend just asked you to do a 90-minute talk tomorrow at 9 a.m. in front of 200 of your ideal prospects, could you come up with 10 topics?

Think of these topics as key points you want to talk about.

Example

Assume you're writing a book on selling. The book's title is *How to Become a Sales Superstar*.

These are sample topics you could use:

1. Closing sales
2. Prospecting
3. Handling objections
4. Attitude
5. Rapport
6. Dress
7. Networking
8. Setting goals
9. Getting a coach
10. Time management
11. Enthusiasm
12. Product knowledge
13. Advertising
14. Follow-up
15. Lead management

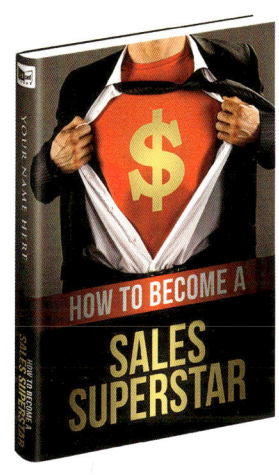

Exercise 1

Write 15 Chapter Titles (Major Topics)

Write down 15 topics in any order.

✓ Chapter 1: TRAIN YOUR MIND MUSCLE
✓ Chapter 2: AGE IS JUST A #
✓ Chapter 3: YOUR PAST DOES NOT DEFINE YOU.
✓ Chapter 4: REWARD YOURSELF C SEX
✓ Chapter 5: VIEW EXCERCISE DIFFERENTLY
✓ Chapter 6: STRENGTH TRAIN
Chapter 7: FASTED CARDIO
Chapter 8: LEARN TO RUN
Chapter 9: LEARN TO SWIM LIKE A PRO
✓ Chapter 10: YOU ARE FAT! OWN IT!
Chapter 11: EATING CLEAN VS DIRTY
✓ Chapter 12: FUEL THE MACHINE (THE SCIENCE)
Chapter 13: MEDITATE
Chapter 14: LOVE YOURSELF
✓ Chapter 15: MAKE IT FUN

Step 2: Cut the 15 to 10 Chapter Titles and Place in Sequence

An AWESOME start. Now drop five topics and put the remainder in logical sequence. In our sales book example, you wouldn't write about 'closing' a sale before you wrote about 'prospecting'.

The sequence and the topics themselves may change as you work on your blueprint. Why? Because you are going to...

Get it DOWN, then get it RIGHT!

Let go of the need to be PERFECT!
If this is taking you longer than 10 minutes – YOU ARE THINKING TOO MUCH!

Back to our example of the book on *How to Become a Sales Superstar*...

1. Attitude
2. Setting goals
3. Advertising
4. Prospecting
5. Networking
6. Rapport
7. Handling objections
8. Closing sales
9. Time management
10. Follow-up

Exercise 2

Your Major Topics in Sequence

Having crossed off five topics now, put the remaining 10 in sequence.

Chapter 1: Your Past Does Not Define You.

Chapter 2: Age Is Just A #

Chapter 3: Train Your Mind Muscle.

Chapter 4: You Are Fat

Chapter 5: View Excercise Differently

Chapter 6: Reward Yourself c Sex

Chapter 7: Do A Triathlon

Chapter 8: Fuel The Machine (The Science)

Chapter 9: Strength Train

Chapter 10: Make It Fun

Step 3: Write 18 Ingredients for Each Chapter

Now you have 10 chapters for your book. To begin writing, you need to take each chapter and figure out what you are going to include. The first thing you need to do is to ask yourself: What are the ingredients that will go into this chapter? You can view these as subtitles or subtopics in this chapter. Just like baking a cake. For this step, come up with 18. Force yourself to come up with 18. Why 18? Because I said so. When you are making more money than me, do it your way! Until then, do it my way! LOL!

Example

Continuing on in our pretend book on sales, one chapter is on Attitude. Here are some ingredients that could go into that chapter:

1. Self-esteem
2. Self-confidence
3. Happiness
4. Old programming
5. Letting go of the past
6. Enthusiasm
7. Personal development
8. Education
9. Getting a coach
10. Goal-setting
11. Exercise
12. Nutrition
13. Laughter
14. Stress-relief
15. Balance
16. Trust
17. Celebration
18. Helping others

Exercise 3

Write 18 Ingredients. These are subtopics or supporting ideas.

Ingredient 1: _____

Ingredient 2: _____

Ingredient 3: _____

Ingredient 4: _____

Ingredient 5: _____

Ingredient 6: _____

Ingredient 7: _____

Ingredient 8: _____

Ingredient 9: _____

Ingredient 10: _____

Ingredient 11: _____

Ingredient 12: _____

Ingredient 13: _____

Ingredient 14: _____

Ingredient 15: _____

Ingredient 16: _____

Ingredient 17: _____

Ingredient 18: _____

Step 4: Cut 18 Chapter Ingredients to 15 and Put Them in Sequence

Remove three ingredients so you are left with 15 and put them in sequence.

1. Letting go of the past
2. Old programming
3. Self-esteem
4. Exercise
5. Self-confidence
6. Laughter
7. Happiness
8. Enthusiasm
9. Personal development
10. Education
11. Getting a coach
12. Goal-setting
13. Nutrition
14. Stress-relief
15. Balance

Robert's Rules on Writing

Your book will be done when you decide to have it done. Decide right now what hours you will set aside to write your book. Lock those hours into your calendar. Do not let anything or anyone distract you from spending those hours on your book.

Exercise 4

15 Chapter Ingredients in Sequence

Ingredient 1: _____

Ingredient 2: _____

Ingredient 3: _____

Ingredient 4: _____

Ingredient 5: _____

Ingredient 6: _____

Ingredient 7: _____

Ingredient 8: _____

Ingredient 9: _____

Ingredient 10: _____

Ingredient 11: _____

Ingredient 12: _____

Ingredient 13: _____

Ingredient 14: _____

Ingredient 15: _____

"You don't get your goals… you get your MUSTS!"

— *Tony Robbins*

Step 5: Turn Ingredients into 15 Significant Statements

Now, turn the 15 ingredients into 15 significant statements. Energize, emotionalize or expand each ingredient. What you want to do is put some emotional "umph" to each.

Ingredient	Significant Statement
1. Letting Go of the Past	"Forget yesterday and fly into a sales explosion."
2. Old Programming	"Grab the old programming by the throat."
3. Self-Esteem	"Be the sunshine you are already."
4. Exercise	"Don't poop out; pop up daily."
5. Self-Confidence	"You've got to believe in yourself to win in sales."
6. Laughter	"Lighten up, will ya?"
7. Happiness	"Sour pusses need not apply."
8. Enthusiasm	"Put some bounce in your step and it will translate to $ in your pocket."
9. Personal Development	"The highest income earners are the best learners."
10. Education	"How to get a degree in your car!"
11. Getting a Coach	"A good coach is worth his/her weight in gold."
12. Goal-Setting	"You can't hit a target you can't see."
13. Nutrition	"Eat your way to great sales success."
14. Stress-Relief	"You deserve a break today."
15. Balance	"Keep it together, man!"

Exercise 5

15 Significant Statements

Take each ingredient and ask yourself: "What is significant about this ingredient?" Make a very brief statement about each ingredient.

1: _____

2: _____

3: _____

4: _____

5: _____

6: _____

7: _____

8: _____

9: _____

10: _____

11: _____

12: _____

13: _____

14: _____

15: _____

Step 6: Turn Each Significant Statement into a Question

Turn each significant statement into a question. Ask, "Why?" or "How?" or "What is the best way to..." Any question that will elicit some answer for you is great. Remember the theme here? "Get it DOWN, then get it RIGHT!"

1. Significant Statement: "Forget yesterday and fly into a sales explosion."
   Question: What is the best way to forget yesterday?

2. Significant Statement: "Grab the old programming by the throat."
   Question: Why should salespeople grab the old programming?

3. Significant Statement: "Be the sunshine you are already."
   Question: How can you release the sunshine you have inside?

4. Significant Statement: "Don't poop out; pop up daily."
   Question: How can you not poop out in selling?

5. Significant Statement: "You've got to believe in yourself to win in sales."
   Question: Why do you have to believe in yourself to win in sales?

6. Significant Statement: "Lighten up, will ya?"
   Question: What prevents people from laughing more?

7. Significant Statement: "Sour pusses need not apply."
   Question: What's the problem with sour pusses in selling?

8. Significant Statement: "Put some bounce in your step and it will translate to $ in your pocket."
   Question: How does enthusiasm translate to $$$ in your pocket?

9. Significant Statement: "The highest income earners are the best learners."
   Question: Why are the highest income earners the best learners?

10. Significant Statement: "How to get a degree in your car!"
    Question: What are the advantages of self-education?

11. Significant Statement: "A good coach is worth his/her weight in gold."
Question: Why is a good coach worth his/her weight in gold?

12. Significant Statement: "You can't hit a target you can't see."
Question: What are three problems with having no goals for salespeople?

13. Significant Statement: "Eat your way to great sales success."
Question: What are the three reasons people in sales eat such crappy food and what can they do about it?

14. Significant Statement: "You deserve a break today."
Question: How can you implement habits that relieve stress?

15. Significant Statement: "Keep it together, man!"
Question: What are the dangers of being out of balance as a salesperson?

Step 7: Come Up with Three Answers for Each Question

This whole book will actually be written by answering these questions.

You will write for five minutes for each answer. If you add that all up, it translates to:

FIVE minutes per answer, times three per ingredient, times 15 ingredients, times 10 chapters = 40 hours!

Answer Words

What happens when someone asks you a question? Your automatic and immediate response is to answer the question. Answer words are the trigger that start the creative writing process.

As you read the question and the three answer words, you will begin to write on the topic just as if someone had asked you the question. The significant statement is a right brain, creative approach. The question triggers your left brain, logical thought process. You can't help it. You have to answer the question.

Time to start writing – just answer your questions.

Take the first question and answer it. Your answer could start with one of the answer words and should use all three answer words.

Write for five minutes and stop.

Do not write longer than five minutes to answer any question. If you have more to say on a question, then make it two or three ingredients (topics).

Be sure you take it through the… ingredient… statement… question… three-answer-word sequence.

Five minutes of writing will produce about 200 typed words or 2/3 of a page of handwriting. If you follow this process, you will have a chapter written in 75 minutes.

Warning

This process is deceptively easy. You may decide to take a more complicated route – it's your book – go ahead, BUT if you want to produce a well-written first draft, stay with the plan. Or visit: www.publishabookandgrowrich.com.

No Shortcuts

One of the sayings attributed to Abraham Lincoln is: "If I had 30 minutes to cut down a tree, I would spend the first 25 minutes sharpening my axe."

The time you spend on your plan – your 15 ingredients, 15 statements, 15 questions, and three answer words – is you sharpening your axe. You will be amazed at how quickly and smoothly the words will flow once you have your plan in place. You will also be amazed at the quality of the end result.

Why Is It So Simple?

Essentially, you are answering questions. Imagine that a friend is sitting across the desk from you asking each question. Could you answer him or her? If someone asked you if goals should be in writing, could you give them an immediate answer? Could you expound on goal-setting for five minutes?

Write as If You Were Talking!

Don't use five-dollar words – you will lose most of your readers. Keep your sentences short. You want your book to be natural. You want it to sound as if the reader was sitting across the table from you, asking you the questions in your outline.

Robert's Rules on Writing

The more deadlines you give yourself, the more productive you'll become.

FREE OFFER

Scan this QR code or visit
www.publishabookandgrowrich.com/wab
to download an Excel spreadsheet called
Write A Book Worksheet for FREE.
It's perfect for those people who prefer to type.

I also suggest you 'plant' people within the content of your book. If you want to meet certain people or get appointments with certain companies or their CEO, say something favourable about them in your book then send them a copy. I guarantee it will change their perception of you and it will significantly increase the likelihood that they will grant you an appointment to meet up.

Plant AMDs or AMEs (Attraction Marketing Devices or Events)

You always want to offer FREE things in your book to cause people to go to your website and give you their contact details so that you can market to them in the future. Here's a small list of things to offer to your readers:

- FREE Seminar Tickets
- FREE Home Study Course
- FREE Consultation (Don't use this if everyone in your industry already offers this)
- FREE Test
- FREE Quiz
- FREE 2nd Opinion
- FREE Cheat Sheet
- FREE Pocket Guide
- FREE Email Course
- FREE Documents (contracts, letters, agreements, etc.)
- FREE Toolkit
- FREE Email Coaching
- FREE Flowchart
- FREE Action Guide
- FREE Comparison Sheet
- FREE Teleseminar
- FREE Webinar
- FREE Transcript

MILLENNIALS you CAN CREATE the Life and Business You Want!

You can get the career as an entrepreneur that you love, the life you want, and feel absolutely amazing by being yourself through a non-traditional way that works for you! Build a business and career aligned with your true purpose in life, and finally have the outcome you have always wanted.

With Anastasia Button's simple coaching processes and tools, you will identify your authentic self, purpose, and desires. Your entrepreneurship will flow easily through strategic networking, mentorship, education, follow through, and a great support system.

- Develop tools to plow through personal and professional obstacles you have battled for years.
- Learn to find the people who will get what you want faster.
- Learn to be a top performer in your industry with high profits.
- Develop harmony in your personal and professional life that will work hand-in-hand.

— TIPS —

1 **How can you get more sales and gain more customers?** Be authentic! How? Bring your energy and focus away from your brain and mind. Breathe. Push the energy down below the bellybutton and to the back of the spine. This is your authentic-core space. When you are no longer in your mind but in your body, you are in unison. Your thoughts, mind, and feelings are one and everything is natural.

2 **How can you be more proficient in your business?** Your business is an extension of you, the entrepreneur! If your business is dysfunctional, not profitable or unorganized then look at yourself; most likely you are brining your own fears from personal past experiences. Remedy with asking why. Why do I feel I need to… Why do I want… Asking why will lead you to understanding how you believe in yourself.

3 **Save time and money with this simple thing:** Your mission statement. Why are you in business? What brought you, the entrepreneur, to offer your services or products? Why is having this business of product or service so important to you? Make one or two statements. Your business partners, employees and customers want to know why they should choose you over others. Give it to them in your mission statement and marketing. If you do not have an authentic mission statement then your business is working harder than it needs to and will suffer in the end.

4 **How to get more results, faster!** Entrepreneurs love to think they can do an unimaginable amount of work and by themselves. You are the heart of the business but it takes a body of people to make the business move at top speeds. Allow people into your business, whether they are in collaboration or gaining responsibility. You are only one person; have an army or network behind you to fuel your success.

5 **How can you take your business to the next level?** Even though you are an entrepreneur, you are still human and humans need balance. Doing consistent hours throughout the week allows time for personal and recreational time. Schedule time for work and bust it out hardcore, then take the time to enjoy the life you are working so hard for!

ANASTASIA BUTTON
MILLENNIAL COACH | AUTHOR | SPEAKER

As a Millennial herself, Anastasia felt the pain of working one undesirable job after another, and the disappointment of what the world has to offer when lifestyle is compromised because there is no "career."

After many years of feeling unhappy and unable to make the right decisions, she was days away from starting graduate school overseas when she thought, "I want travel, adventure, fun, and to use my mind to make a large income. **There has to be a better and more authentic way to get what I want."**

Deciding to take her life into her own hands, Anastasia began being authentic to her core-self and became an entrepreneur. The decision wasn't easy and the actions were difficult where many fears, obstacles, and barriers were hurdled, but Anastasia was still not making progress and living the life she wanted.

Finally, after a year of not making any money, Anastasia discovered that in order to have a business that doesn't survive but **THRIVE**, she needed to be completely authentic and work on her inner demons, fears, and insecurities to obtain the life she wanted. "We don't fit in a cookie cutter. We work differently, think differently, and aim for the stars!" Identifying how you work as an individual is the key to making the entrepreneur thrive and the business will easily follow afterwards. Speaking to groups and coaching clients, Anastasia shows others how they can have what they want in life and business.

Scan this to find out more!

ready to get started?
ANASTASIABUTTON.COM
+1 720 232 5988 | Anastasia@AnastasiaButton.com

Get a FREE 90-minute coaching session!

FREE CONSULTATION

These Black Card Books authors attended my Publish a Book & Grow Rich bootcamp:

GET YOUR FREE* TICKET HERE

www.publishabookandgrowrich.com/freeticket

*Not applicable in every country.

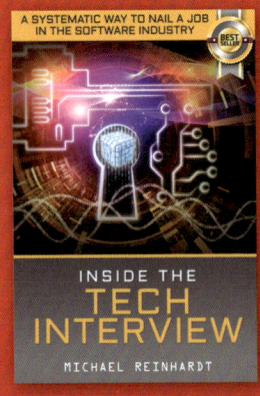
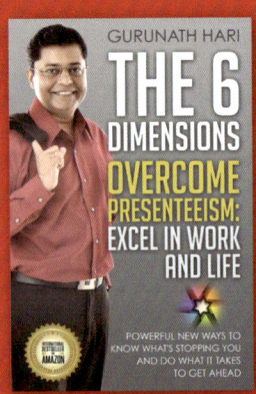
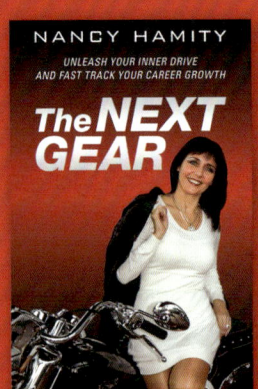

PLAN IT
WRITE IT
PUBLISH IT
FUND IT
MOVE IT

Chapter Three

Sell People What They Want but Give Them What They Need.

3

PUBLISH IT

All the Boring Technical Stuff about How to Get a Book That Will Rock Your World.

- Write a Killer Title.
- Covers That Stop People in Their Tracks and Compel Them to Read Your Book.
- The Ins and Outs of Production… Become a Publishing Expert in 40 Minutes (which is about how long it will take you to read this part).
- How I Got Major Celebrity Endorsements/Forewords, and How You Can Too – It's Easy with My Secret Trick.

> "Since most people purchase books based on the principle of self-interest, the key to powerful marketing is to show how you meet other people's needs. Therefore your promotional efforts should be audience-focused, rather than self-focused. All of your book markcting materials, such as your website, back cover copy, personal bio, bookmarks, newsletters, and even social media posts, should explain how you can improve a reader's life."

— Rob Eagar, author of *Sell Your Book Like Wildfire: The Writer's Guide to Marketing and Publicity*

Nail Your Title

How to come up with a title that sizzles so much that people are instantly attracted to you and your book, and that they absolutely MUST pick it up, buy it or call you!

Okay, that's a little overkill on the headline for this, but the title of a book, like the headline of an advertisement or news story, often makes the difference between a reader passing by the book or picking it up and giving it more careful consideration. More often than not, the reader gives less than a moment's attention to any book title and if you don't capture the reader's imaqination or curiosity or desire in that short moment, you will have lost the sale.

Below are a few suggestions on how you can create titles that will help you accomplish your P.O. (Primary Objective):

Shock

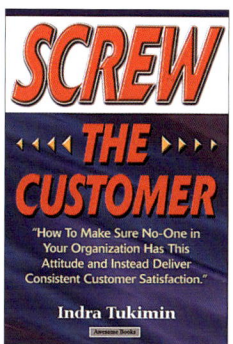

We had an author choose *Screw the Customer* as a way to shock people to look deeper into the book. It was a great title. Which book reviewer could pass this up? It was subtitled, "How To Make Sure No-One in Your Organization Has This Attitude"... something the author's T.POP. was keenly interested in.

Test Your Titles Beforehand

Some authors have gone to shopping malls and bookstores to ask for feedback from people they met. While this is an informal testing method, it can provide you with some valuable feedback about your title and your book.

Be Specific

Let the readers know what they can expect to get from your book. Specific benefits are usually more effective than general benefits in appealing to book buyers.

Use Controversy If You Possibly Can!

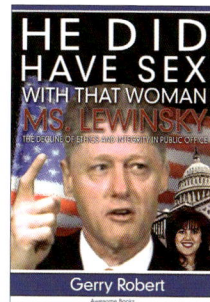

I wrote *He Did Have Sex with THAT Woman... Miss Lewinsky!...* but for numerous reasons, it was never published. The only reason I liked it was because of the press I would have received. I also timed it to come out at the same time as the former president's book.

> "My first rule is that titles must be memorable. This is crucial, since 80 percent of books are sold by word of mouth. If people can't remember a title, they can't pass it on."
>
> — John Kremer, author of *1001 Ways to Market Your Book*

Use Subtitles

Use subtitles to provide further explanation or description of the book's contents or benefits. Here are two Black Card Books examples of superb benefit subtitles:

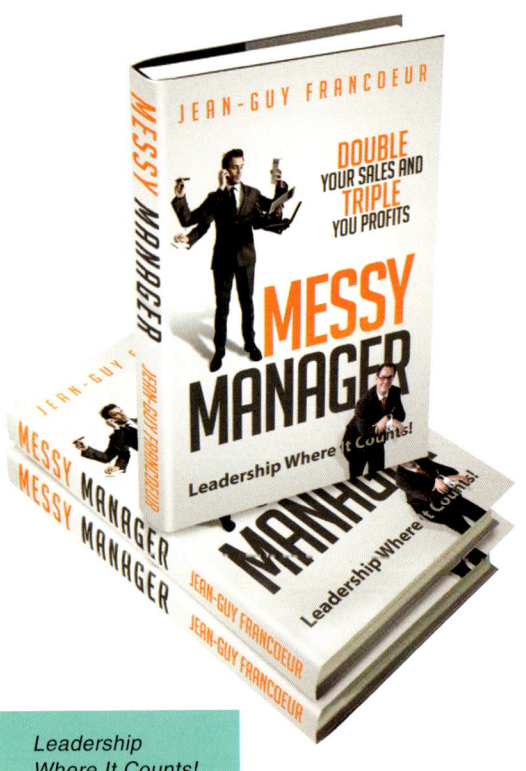

Leadership Where It Counts!

Download a copy of this book.

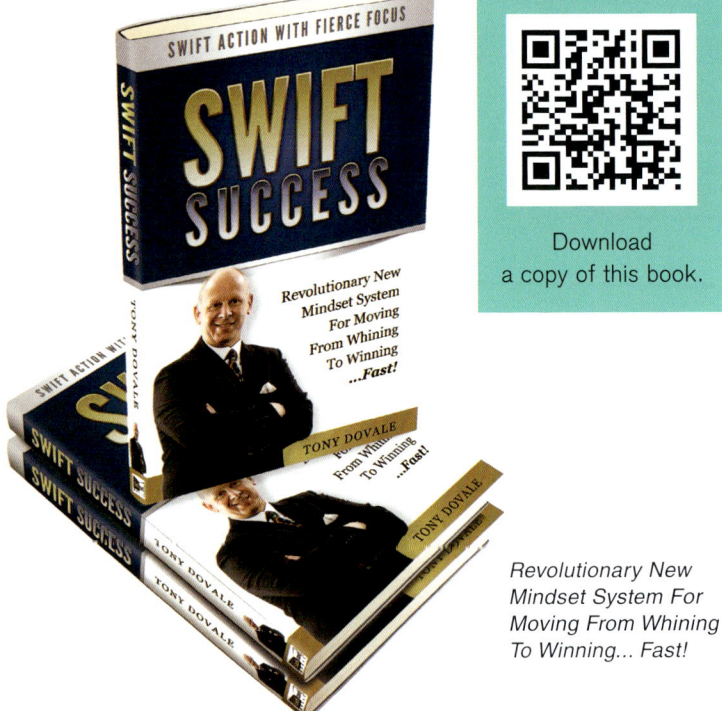

Download a copy of this book.

Revolutionary New Mindset System For Moving From Whining To Winning... Fast!

Choose Titles That Play Off the Titles of Other Well-Known Books

Major Mohan, one of the authors in our Author Mentorship Program, wrote a great book, which he titled *Think Network Marketing & Grow Rich*, playing off the famous book by Napoleon Hill.

Choose Familiar Lead-Ins to Your Titles

For example, *The Joy of Sex*, *The Joy of Working Out*, *The Joy of Cooking*, *The Joy of Photography*, *The Joy of Publishing*, and so on.

Or, that classic book title lead-in:

How to… do just about anything. Or, finally, how about 101 Ways to… do just about anything?

"It's not the book, it's the HOOK."
— *Joel Roberts*

Make It Pronounceable

If you expect to do interviews, make sure the title is easy to pronounce.

Make It Memorable

When John Gray followed up his bestselling *Men Are from Mars, Women Are from Venus* with *What Your Mother Couldn't Tell You and Your Father Didn't Know*, Borders bookstore returned 50% and Ingram, 70%. Why? Because the second book didn't have nearly as memorable a title.

Title Checklist

You can do this!

The following checklist has many ideas that have worked for authors the world over. Use this checklist to compare the title you are thinking about.

Is the Title Specific?

Does it say *Make Money from Home* when you really mean *Make Money from Facebook*?

Is the Title Attention-Grabbing Enough?

Is your title flat and boring? *Dating 101* hardly sold. Once the author changed the title (and only the title) to *Nice Guys Don't Get Laid*, he sold 300,000 copies in the next 12 months.

Does Your Title Offer Strong Benefits That Are Client-Centered?

Does your title simply say *Recovering from Being Fired* instead of promising readers *How to Find Your Dream Job in 60 Days or Less – Even If You've Been Fired*?

Will Readers Know What You Mean?

Does the title use obscure terms, like *Codependency and Intimacy: A Female Perspective*, or is it stated in a language anyone can recognize, like *Women Who Love Too Much*?

Is Your Title Consistent with Your P.O. (Primary Objective)?

"Improperly capitalizing the title and subtitle. Use headline-style capitalization for titles and subtitles. This means capitalizing the first word, last word, and every noun, pronoun, verb, adjective, and adverb. Start articles, prepositions shorter than five letters, and conjunctions with lowercase letters. Contrary to popular belief, headline style does not mean lowercasing all 'small' words. Some small words are verbs ('Is', 'Are', and 'Be') are prime examples or other parts of speech aside from prepositions."

— Guy Kawasaki and Shawn Welch, authors of *APE: Author, Publisher, Entrepreneur - How to Publish a Book*

Book Title Primer

Use the list below to help you come up with a title for your book:

Do You Make Any of These Mistakes…

The Quickest Way to…

The 5 Sure-Fire Ways to…

How You Can Make a Fortune

How to Pay Less for…

Amazing Money-Making Ideas

Why Some People Always Succeed in…

101 Things to Help You…

Now, at Last, UNLOCK the Secrets to…

The Amazing Secrets of a… Superstar Now Revealed!

Easy Ways to…

How to… and Get More…

What Everyone Ought to Know Before Buying…

Where the Money Is and How to Get It

… Expert Discovers…

How to… for Under…

How to Get FREE…

This Book Can Make You $… Richer

How to Increase Your… by… %

How to Sell More Goods and Services to More People, More Quickly and Most Cost Effectively than Ever

How to Increase… while Reducing…

The 10 Most Common Mistakes Everyone Makes while…

Wealth without…

5 Innovative Concepts That Will Boost Your Bottom-Line Profits by 44%-300% within One Year – GUARANTEED!

10 Quick-Fix Solutions for an Ailing…

Write Your Own Ticket to…

POWER CHARGE Your…

CHARGE UP Your…

Liberate Yourself from…

Secrets of Investing That Are 100 Times More Successful than What You Have Now

How to Instantly DOUBLE the Amount of Money You Earn at Work

29 Things That Make an Incredible Difference to Your…

Find Out about the New Way to… and Save… or Make…

Unemployed? Get to Work FAST!

Single? Sincere? Serious?

The 6 Most Costly… Mistakes

WARNING! WARNING! WARNING! Don't Even Think about… Until You Read This Book

You Can Have a Highly Organized, Efficient, Low-Stress, HIGHLY Profitable Practice Easier, Quicker, and More Affordable than You Might Think

Let Me Show You How You Can Easily Have the Life YOU Want

Dispelling the Myths of…

If I Give You a Dollar You Would Never Have Had, Would You Give Me Back a Quarter?

If You Ever Wanted to Know about…

Norman Vincent Peale Wrote a Book Called *The Power of Positive Thinking*. HE WAS WRONG!

Forget Everything Your Mother Told You about…

Shocking New Discovery Reveals…

Life Stinks!!! Especially When Your (blank) Is Unreliable

Find Out What to Do the Next Time It…

OH MY GOSH! Not Another…

Discover the Secrets That Will Guarantee You Retire Rich, Even If You Work at a Low-Paying Job for Your Entire Life

14 Easy-to-Use Techniques to Ensure You Never Get Ripped Off by a… (occupation)

Fast, Easy, and Reliable Methods to Give You…

Roses Are Red, Violets Are Blue. Buy Her Some… and There'll Be Kisses for You

… Ways to Accomplish…

22 Ways to Profit in a Down Market

Apply These 8 Secret Techniques to Improve…

Believing These 8 Myths about… Keeps You from…

Don't Waste Time!

8 Facts to…

… Doesn't Have to Be Hard

… Is Your Worst Enemy

Get… on a Budget

Master the Art of…

My Life, My Job, My Career: 8 Simple Career Techniques That Helped Me Succeed

The Next 8 Things You Should Do If You Want…

Time Is Running Out!

Think about These 8 Ways to Change Your…

The 8 Biggest… Mistakes You Can Easily Avoid

Think Your… Is Safe?
8 Ways You Can Lose It Today

Thinking about… 8 Reasons Why It's Time to Stop!

8 Creative Ways You Can Improve…

8 Easy Steps to Get More…

8 Effective Ways to Get More Out of…

8 Facts Everyone Should Know about…

8… Mistakes That Will Cost You $… over the Next 10 Years

8 Life-Saving Tips about…

8 Little Known Ways to Make the Most Out of…

8 Most Well-Guarded Secrets about…

8 Questions You Need to Ask before You Buy…

8 Ridiculously Simple Ways to Improve Your…

8 Secrets about… They Are Still Keeping from You

8 Simple Ways the Pros Use to Promote…

8 Solid Reasons to Avoid…

8 Steps to… of Your Dreams

8 Facts You Didn't Know about…

8 Super Useful Tips to Improve…

8 Surprisingly Effective Ways to…

8 Things to Demystify…

8 Things You Can Learn from Buddhist Monks about…

8 Things You Didn't Know about…

8 Things You Have in Common with…

8 Things You Must Know about…

8 Things Your Mom Should Have Taught You about…

8 Tips about… You Can't Afford to Miss

8 Tips for… Success

8 Tips That Will Make You a Guru in…

8 Tips to Reinvent Your… and Win

8 Tips to Start Building a… You Always Wanted

8 Tricks about… You Wish You Knew Before

Cracking the… Secret… Secrets Revealed

Secrets Your Parents Never Told You about…

The Hidden Mystery Behind…

The… Mystery

The Secret Behind…

The Secret Guide to…

The Secret History of…

The Secret Life of…

The Secret of…

The Truth about… in 3 Little Words

The Ultimate Secret of…

8… Secrets You Never Knew

What Everyone Ought to Know about…

You, Me, and… the Truth

8 Reasons… Is a Waste of Time

Beware the… Scam

Don't Be Fooled by…

How to Deal with a Very Bad…

How to Lose Money with…

How to Slap Down a…

In 10 Minutes, I'll Give You the Truth about…

… Smackdown!

Lies and Damn Lies about…

Rules Not to Follow about…

Slacker's Guide to…

The Lazy Man's Guide to…

The Mafia Guide to…

8 Mistakes in… That Make You Look Dumb

8 Myths about…

8 Ridiculous Rules about…

8 Rules about… Meant to Be Broken

8 Surefire Ways… Will Drive Your Business into the Ground

Why I Hate…

Why Most… Fail

Why My… Is Better than Yours

Why You Never See a… That Actually Works

Fascinating… Tactics That Can Help Your Business Grow

How to Get… for under $100

How to Make Your Product the Ferrari of…

How to Start a Business with Only…

… Is Bound to Make an Impact on Your Business

… Strategies for the… Challenged

Listen to Your Customers. They Will Tell You All about…

One Word:...

Prioritizing Your... to Get the Most out of Your Business

Pump Up Your Sales with These Remarkable ... Tactics

The Simple... That Wins Customers

8 Easy Steps to a Winning... Strategy

8 Incredibly Useful... for Small Businesses

8 Tips for Using... to Leave Your Competition in the Dust

8 Unforgivable Sins of...

8 Unheard-Of Ways to Achieve Greater...

8 Very Simple Things You Can Do to Save...

8 Warning Signs of Your... Demise

8 Ways to Create Better... With the Help of...

8 Ways... Can Make You Invincible

8 Ways to Get through to Your...

8 Ways to Immediately Start Selling...

8 Ways to Keep Your... Growing without Burning the Midnight Oil

8 Ways to Master... without Breaking a Sweat

8 Ways to Reinvent Your...

8 Ways You Can Get More... While Spending Less

8 Ways You Can Reinvent... without Looking like an Amateur

8 Ways You Can Use... to Become Irresistible to Customers

Using 8... Strategies like the Pros

Warning: These 8 Mistakes Will Destroy Your...

The A to Z of…

The Next 70 Things to Immediately Do about…

The Ultimate Guide to…

70 Methods of… Domination

101 Things to Do Immediately about…

70 Tips to Grow Your…

70 Ways to Avoid… Burnout

70 Ways to Improve…

How to Make More… by Doing Less

How to Make…

How to Earn $1,000,000 Using…

How to Become Better with… in 10 Minutes

How to Improve at… in 60 Minutes or Less

How to Handle Every… Challenge with Ease

How to Get a Fabulous… on a Tight Budget

How to Turn Your… from Blah into Fantastic

Is… a Scam?

Sick and Tired of Doing… the Old Way?

Want an Easy Fix for Your…?

What You Ought to Know about…

What… Experts Don't Want You to Know

What Shakespeare Can Teach You about…

What Zombies Can Teach You about…

Where Is the Best…?

Everyone Loves…

Fall in Love with…

8 Ways to Make People Fall in Love with Your Product

Use… to Make…

8 Sexy Ways to Improve Your…

Albert Einstein on…

Being a Rockstar in Your Industry Is a Matter of…

Charlie Sheen's Guide to…

The Mel Gibson Effect…

Cracking the… Code

Death,… and Taxes: Tips on Avoiding…

Fighting for… the Samurai Way

Get Rid of… Problems Once and for All

Here's a Quick Way to Solve the… Problem

… What a Mistake!

… It's Easy If You Do It Smart

Never Lose Your… Again

No More Mistakes with…

The Death of… and How to Avoid It

Warning: What You Can Do about… Right Now

Attention:…

Little Known Facts about… and Why They Matter

The Philosophy of…

Warning:…

Put Some Muscle in Your Table of Contents

Next to your cover and back cover, your Table of Contents is one of the most important elements of your book's marketing muscle. Watch the way people look at books in a bookstore. First, they look at the front cover (8 seconds), then they flip it over and read the back cover (15 seconds), and if they are still interested, they always go to the Table of Contents (TOC). So that page must be written very well and it needs to sell the book to the reader. This is what we call key publishing real estate. Each chapter title must be a mini-ad for your book!

A POOR Table of Contents simply gives the reader basic chapter titles – titles that have no call-to-action and are not motivating to the reader.

Bad TOC

1. Lacks CTA (Call-to-Action).
2. Doesn't say much.
3. Boring.
4. Emotionless.
5. Doesn't know how it solves my pain.
6. Doesn't make you want to instantly find that chapter.

Great TOC

1. Creates excitement.
2. Has an "I've got to learn this now" feel.
3. Grabs your attention.
4. Makes a bold claim.
5. Solves problems.
6. Shows mistakes to avoid.

A GOOD Table of Contents actually motivates the prospective buyer to buy your book – in fact, if you have 10 chapters, you have 10 chances to grab the person's attention and get them to take action and buy your book. I've had many letters come into our office stating the reader bought one of my books just to get the information in a single chapter. However, they went on to read the rest of the book and are now living a more fulfilling life because of what they learned.

The most important thing to learn from this aspect of the program is that every browser is looking for something different – one chapter description may motivate 100 people to buy but not do anything to motivate the next 1,000. If you have a compelling description beside each chapter, you'll sell far more books.

Put Power in Your Cover

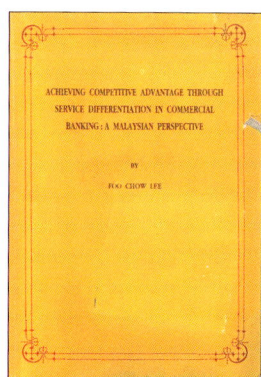
BEFORE

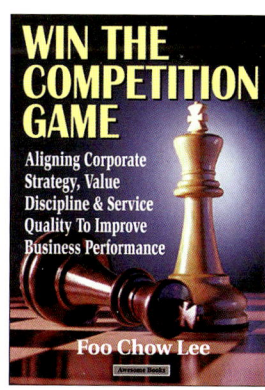
AFTER

I was doing a seminar in Malaysia and a management consultant approached me with this godawful cover. I asked him if his book helped him grow his practice any. He hung his head down and muttered, "No." I was not surprised.

He attended my bootcamp and, subsequently, I decided to publish his book. We redesigned his cover to this. I'm not certain but I would guess that this one is a tiny wee bit better. Wouldn't you agree? Your cover makes a big difference to the effectiveness of your book and its ability to grow your business or boost your income.

What's a person like you doing on a cover like that?

The old maxim that you can't judge a book by its cover does not hold true in the real world.

That's precisely how people judge a book.

Go to any bookstore and watch what people do. First, they look at the cover. If it appeals to them, they flip the book over and look at the back for benefits and testimonials, and what the book will deliver. People do judge a book by its cover – not only readers, but also major decision-makers. I've met chain store buyers, wholesale buyers, and even television producers, and I've watched them as they pick up a new book to make a decision.

Within two to three seconds, they've already made their decision. You can see it in their eyes. And all they've done is look at the title, look at the cover and size up the packaging. That's it.

Judith Clinton of Tor Books once observed, "We believe that the cover is a point-of-purchase advertisement of major importance in the marketing of the book."

Elements of Fabulous Cover Designs

"This is the secret: Many people will buy a book without ever seeing the content. They just need one convincing reason to buy. As the author, you can create persuasive reasons that tip the buying scale in your favor."

— Rob Eagar, author of *Sell Your Book Like Wildfire: The Writer's Guide to Marketing and Publicity*

The basic rule of cover design is that the cover should match the contents of the book. That means that the style, format and message of the cover should be compatible with and support the style, format and message of the book itself.

Winner of the Terrible Cover Award

Notice the grammatical error?

Use an Eye-Catching Photo

It doesn't cost any more money to print a nice full-colour picture on your cover, so find one that is outstanding. Remember, you cannot 'borrow' images from the Internet without approval. There are many stock photo websites for you to purchase an impressive image for the cover of your book.

Pain Focus Can Be Good

People today are hurting. Research has shown that people will often respond to advertisements that focus on pain rather than gain. Highlighting something negative is often an effective tool to get their attention.

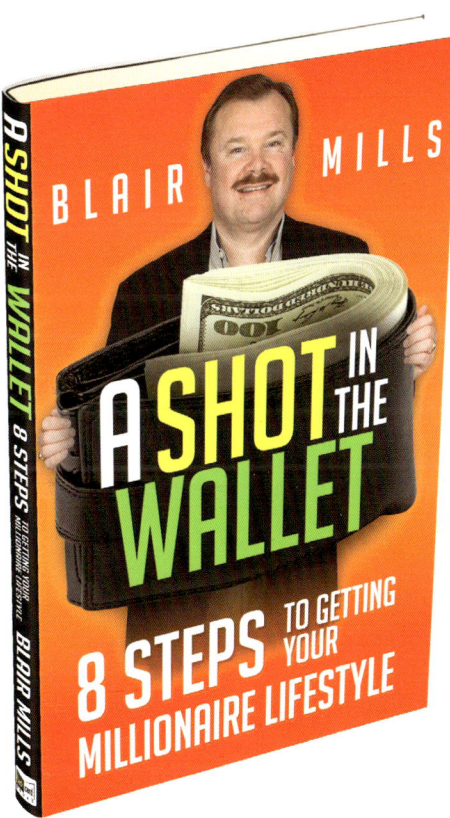

Gain Points Are Good Too

One thing you can do is make the main title positive (Gain Statement) and make the subtitle negative (Pain Statement). This hits both sides of someone's brain.

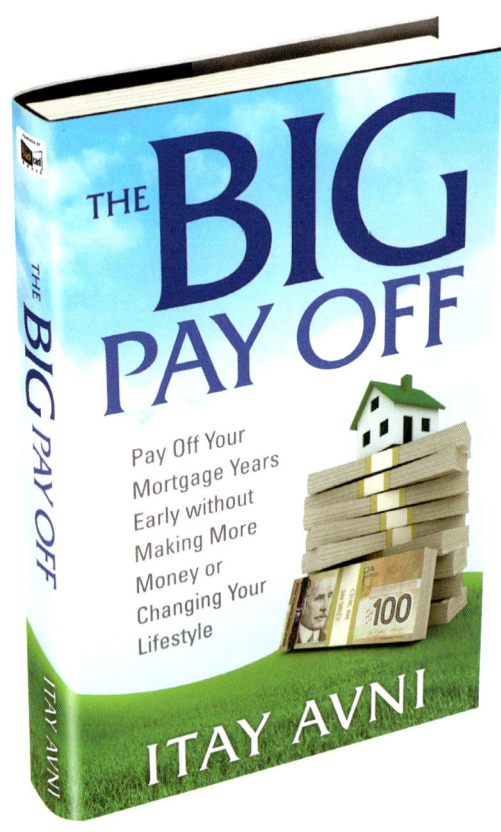

Offer an Ultimate Promise

Since you offer solutions to people's problems in your book, make sure that somewhere in the title or somewhere on the cover, you offer a huge promise. What's the big benefit of reading this book?

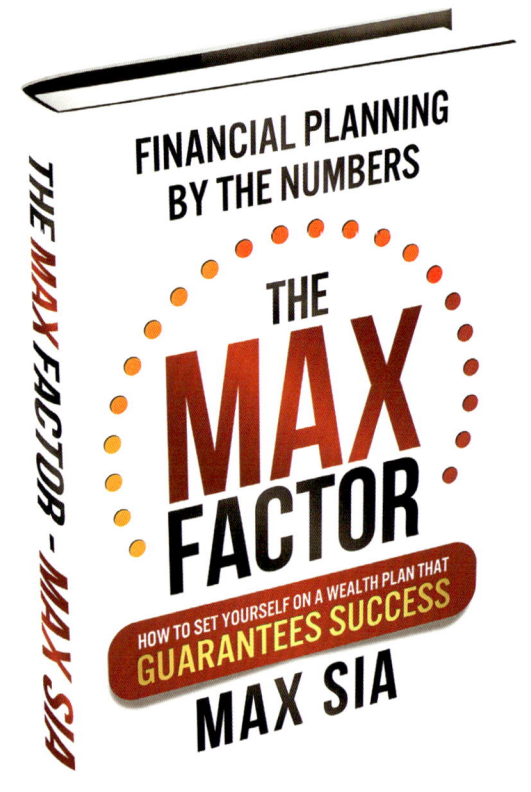

You Could Ask a Question, Couldn't You?

Questions are good for engagement. They often cause people to stop and think.

Be Funny If You Can!

It's not always appropriate but when you cause people to laugh, it grabs their attention, like this book written about the founder of the low-carbs diet craze, Dr. Atkins.

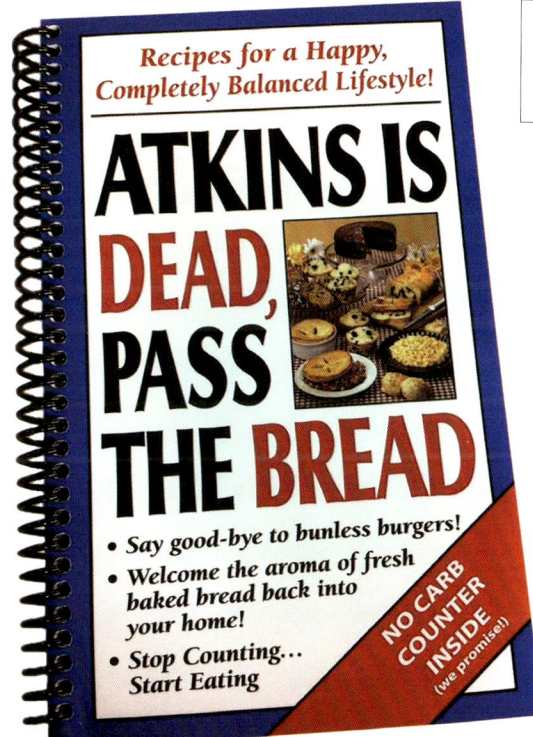

"Not published by me!"

In the next example, I published this book on a serious topic but dealt with in a lighthearted manner on the cover.

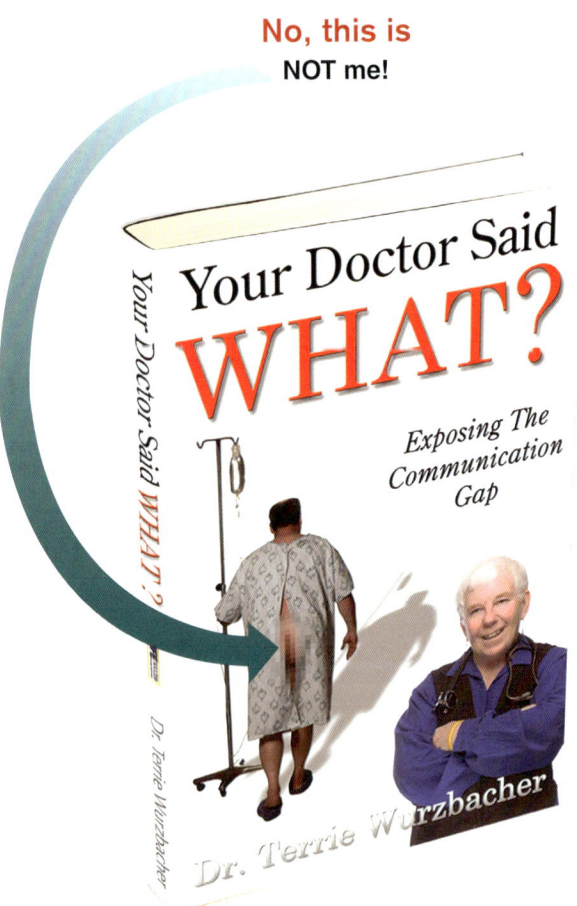

No, this is NOT me!

Consider Using a Strong Author Picture

Since most of you will be using your book to promote yourself, then your picture on the cover as the author is recommended. Make sure that picture, however, shows you in a very strong and powerful light. Sell yourself visually.

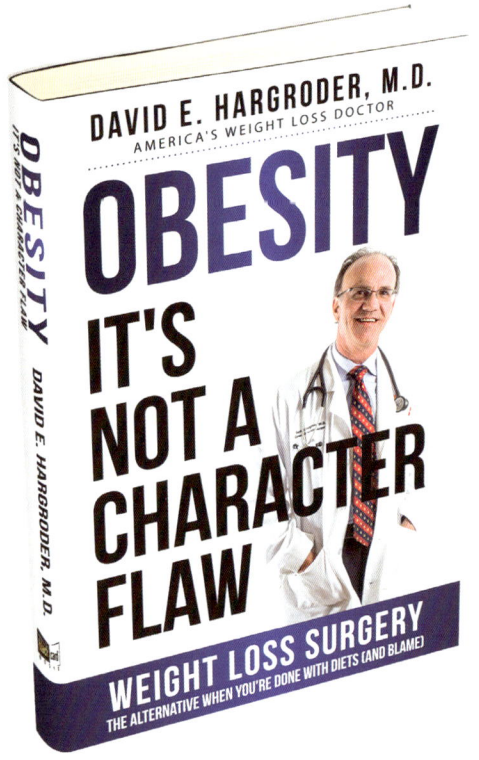

Use Reader-Appropriate Colours

If you know you are selling primarily to women, perhaps you should have different colours on the cover than if you were selling to men. The same applies to teenagers versus parents, or CEOs versus salespeople. It might not be an issue for you, but consider it anyway.

Can You Raise Curiosity Somehow?

By making a certain statement, you cause people to reflect on the title. It stops them for a second or two. Sometimes, that's all you need to get them to check you and your book out more. *The Honest CEO?* Is there such an animal?

Don't Be Ambigious

Make sure that people know exactly what your book is about when they read your cover. There can be no question in their minds after reading your cover when it comes to the topic and even who the book is intended for.

Consider Using a 2nd Subtitle

More and more at Black Card Books, we are using secondary subtitles. This is used to provide even more information about what the book is about, what it will deliver or for whom the book applies.

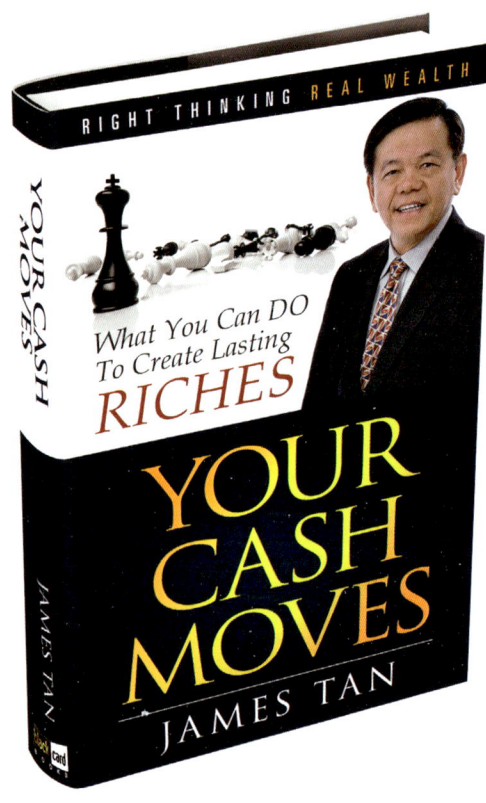

Numbers Often Work Too!

Using numbers often can provide a greater sense of mass to your book. When people see the number 10 or 101, it implies there is a lot of content here.

Use Full Colour

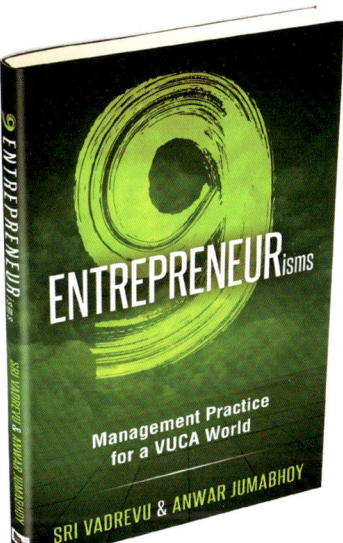

Make sure you use a high-resolution photograph to illustrate your book cover. Any good book designer will know how to obtain stock photos to enhance your book. I've seen people make the front cover black and white but put a full color photo of themselves on the back cover. That's ridiculous! It really wasn't a design issue. I think the author just tried to save some money and it showed.

Make It Stand Out

It must be able to stand out in the crowd. That is one reason Zebra Books printed holograms on the covers of its romance novels. It hoped to distinguish its line of novels so the books stood out on the paperback racks and thereby attracted more attention from potential buyers.

Be Bold and Simple

The front cover of a book should be bold and simple, more like a billboard (which it is) than a full-page display ad. The cover should be uncluttered, easy to read (with highly readable type) and simple enough that the casual browser can catch the title and name of the author without searching for either

Put the Most Important Element at the Top

Generally speaking, the title of the book should be featured at the top of the cover. It's the first thing the reader should see. If, however, the author is well-known and more important than the title, then feature the author's name in bold type at the top of the cover.

Feature Sales Information

Besides the author and title, feature any other information that could be useful in selling the book. Some of our authors have printed an AMD (Attraction Marketing Device) to act as a magnet. Some give away $500 worth of FREE coaching; others give FREE reports or FREE subscriptions to their newsletter.

Never Use Clip Art

It's a sure sign that you are an amateur.

Odd Colours Can Sometimes Work

For example, Rhodes and Easton's *Deer Camp Dictionary*, in its fluorescent-orange cover, sells well in sporting goods shops, gas stations, and other places where hunters congregate.

Avoid Lots of White or Black

Also avoid vast expanses of dark colours. Such colours tend to show fingerprints and other scuffs more vividly. As one bookseller noted, "It's very hard to sell a book with fingerprints on the cover."

Try Different Sizes of Books

101 Productions was the first publisher to use an 8" x 8" format for trade cookbooks, a format that allows for more flexibility in the layout of pages while enabling the book to lie open more easily without breaking the spine. In the past 15 years, 101 has sold more than four million copies of their cookbooks.

1st Place Winner for Crappiest Cover Ever!

Coat the Cover

Besides being your major point-of-purchase advertising for the book, the cover must also protect the book. If it is a paperback book, have the cover varnished, film laminated or coated with a UV plastic. If it is in hardcover, use a jacket (which also allows for a more promotional copy than a cover by itself). Choose lay-flat film lamination over UV coating for paperbacks because UV coating doesn't protect as well.

Test Your Covers

Whenever possible, test your covers with consumers and booksellers. Scribner Publishing sent two versions of a cover for Faye Smith's *Flight of the Blackbird* to 25 African-American booksellers. The cover with a portrait of a family beat out a cover with a blackbird in flight.

Production

It's a lot easier than you think. Here's an overview of the boring stuff:

Printing

Hardcovers (Casebound Books)

Use hardcovers for gift books, library editions, permanent collections, major works of fiction and nonfiction, and professional reference titles.

Hardcovers are still taken more seriously by prospects, customers, potential sponsors, booksellers and reviewers. Hardcovers account for 42% of books sold by warehouse and price clubs, but only 28% of books sold in independent bookstores (where trade paperbacks account for 50% of sales).

Libraries still prefer hardcover editions because they wear better under heavy use. For the same reason, professionals prefer hardcovers for their expensive reference manuals.

Most higher priced books are published in hardcover because such covers are viewed as being more expensive. An exception to this rule, however, are high-priced annual directories, such as *Literary Market Place*, because they are expected to wear out quickly and be replaced with a new edition each year.

Perfect Bound Paperbacks (Softcover)

Use paperbacks for most mass-market titles, inexpensive editions, novelty books, travel guides, poetry, literary novels and any book with an ephemeral topic. According to one study, 58% of all small press titles are now published in trade paperback (also known as quality paperbacks).

Mass market paperbacks are the pocket-sized softcover books sold in drug stores, grocery stores and newsstands. Trade paperbacks are the larger softcover books sold primarily in bookstores.

The main reason to use this format is to keep the retail price down so more readers can afford to buy the book. This might make sense if you plan on giving away thousands of copies of your book as I did for my book, *Multiply Your Business*.

Otabind Paperbacks

This perfect-binding technique can be used for cookbooks, travel guides, software manuals and other books that must lay flat. Using special glue and covers, this system allows a book to lay flat without breaking the binding.

While this form of binding is more expensive than regular perfect binding, it is less expensive than comb binding or spiral binding.

Besides being less expensive than comb or spiral binding, it also ships more readily through the mail. And because it has a spine, it is easier to shelve in bookstores and libraries.

Saddle-Stitched Paperbacks

Use saddle-stitching mainly for workbooks, manuals, reports, newsletters and other expendable publications.

Because saddle-stitched books have no spine and thus cannot be shelved with the spine out, they are hard to sell to libraries and booksellers. Don't use such binding if these are your major markets.

The main value of saddle-stitched books is that they are less expensive to produce. Again, this might make sense if you plan on giving away thousands of copies of your book as I did for my book, *Multiply Your Business*.

The "Innards"

Front Matter

The front and back matter of your books can be used to help market the book. Front matter such as forewords and dedications can help promote the purpose of your book, while back matter such as appendices and bibliographies can increase the resource value of the book and, hence, their marketability. Here's a list of front and back matter which can be used to increase the promotability of your book.

Inside Front Cover (or End Papers)

These may be used for maps, family trees or other illustrations which add to the reader's understanding of a book. Illustrations printed on the inside covers or end papers are easier to refer to while reading.

Half-Title Page

If included at all, this page (the first page in a book) is most often used to list only the title of the book. It may, however, also be used to print additional testimonials and endorsements, or an enticing lead-in paragraph to the story itself.

For example, Warner Books printed a series of questions on the half-title page of the mass market edition of Jerry Gillies' *Moneylove*. If you answered "no" to any of the questions, "you are on the way to discovering the enriching truth about the road to prosperity… and you can get it with *Moneylove*."

Back of the Half-Title Page

If you include a half-title page in your books, use the opposite side to list other books by the author (especially those published by you). It's an inexpensive and unobtrusive way to let readers know about other books by the author.

Title Page

List the title of the book, including any subtitle or explanation; the author, authors, or editor; and the name and logo of your company. Also, list your company's address and phone number, email or website on this page. This will make it easier for readers to find you.

Copyright Page

List the copyright notice, ISBN number, cataloging in publication (CIP) info, and company name and address (if not listed on the previous page). The copyright notice, of course, is required to secure the fullest protection of the copyright law.

The ISBN number allows booksellers and librarians to reorder copies more easily. The CIP information makes it easier for librarians to catalog your books, hence, librarians are more likely to order your books if this information is included. CIP information can be requested from the Library of Congress CIP office (one-book publishers are currently excluded from this program) or from Quality Books, the library distributor. If the book is available in two editions (both hardcover and paperback), print that information on this page as well.

You might want to start a book publishing company; if so, create a name, but it should not be your name with "publishing or books." Make yourself look bigger.

Dedication

This is the soft and mushy part of your book. Include some human interest aspect in your dedications, anything that will speak to the readers and make the dedication more memorable. I dedicated mine to my mentor.

Foreword, Not "Forward"

Yes, it's spelled correctly. It's FOREWORD!

And the person writing it should be known by your T.POP. The foreword to your book could be written by celebrities or by experts on the subject of the book – someone, in short, who will add legitimacy or interest to the book.

For a great summary of Copyright, see this FAQ:
www.blackcardbooks.com/copyright

Preface

The preface should not only establish the author's expertise but also reveal why the author chose to write the book. Many bookstore browsers read the preface before anything else because the preface often reveals the author's motivation for writing the book, gives them insight into the author's style and approach to the subject and provides background on the author and the research behind the book.

Use the preface to establish rapport with the readers of your book. Give them some insight into yourself, your reasons for writing the book and some reason to want to find out more about the subject of the book. Make it personal, and make it interesting.

Acknowledgments

Acknowledgments are a great place to thank those who helped you research and write the book, especially the experts and other resource people who provided the necessary background facts and examples. Such acknowledgments help to establish the reliability of your information.

Each format of your book (hardcover, softcover, eBook and audiobook) requires a unique ISBN.

Endorsements – Foreword

My first book had 26 pages of endorsements. I got Zig Ziglar, Dr. Norman Vincent Peale, Robert Schuller, Ken Blanchard and Rich Devos to write wonderful blurbs for me, an unknown newbie!

The fact is that radio, television and the movies have conditioned the consumer to buy almost anything associated with star power.

Harvey Mackay printed 44 testimonials in *Swim with the Sharks Without Being Eaten Alive*. He had endorsements from everyone – from Billy Graham to Robert Redford. Did these big-name celebs go out and buy a book and write unsolicited testimonials? Of course not. Mackay asked for words of praise.

Testimonials sell books. Why? Because people love to buy by word of mouth, and that's essentially what a testimonial or endorsement is.

I've used testimonials to get sales, introduce me to others, to build my credibility and I did that when I first began in business. The first edition of my first book, *Conquering Life's Obstacles*, had 26 pages of endorsements. I tend to go a little nuts with testimonials. It's easy to do and anyone can do it to gain a significant business advantage.

Testimonials can be one of the most critical elements of your marketing materials. I'd like to show you how to get testimonials, even if you're a new author or just beginning to launch your book.

The bigger the name, the longer lead time you will need in securing the testimonial. Keep that in mind. Without well-written, specific, credible testimonials, it is very difficult to sell anything. You see, you can say all you want about yourself, but the fact is… people DON'T BELIEVE YOU!

They believe what others say much more than they will ever believe you. Testimonials are your 'proof', your expert witnesses in proving the case for your book.

Having a sales pitch without testimonials is like going into court without any witnesses. You can never use too many testimonials, and you should constantly be in the process of collecting them. I can't overstate this enough!

Testimonials Are Your Key Witnesses!

They help you…

- Sell books.

- Give you credibility.

- Make you look important.

- Give you more clout.

- Accrue the value of the testimonial provider to you.

- Become known to the person writing the blurb.

- Get you more sales for your business.

- Get referrals.

- Create more channels of distribution.

I have a file titled 'Testimonials to Add to Next Printing'. I'm constantly asking people for testimonials. (By the way, would YOU please send me one for this book? Email me at cs@blackcardbooks.com.) I keep them on file until the book goes to press again and I always add them to the file.

Too many people use WORTHLESS testimonials that go something like this:

"This book is wonderful!"
— J.B., KL

"Thanks! Great book."
— L.T., Singapore

These kinds of testimonials HURT your credibility more than they help. Keep in mind that the main purpose of a testimonial is to build credibility in you and in your book. Because people are skeptical these days, they will almost always believe what other people have to say about you more than what YOU have to say about yourself.

"This book is wonderful!" J.B., KL, makes the potential buyer wonder (whether consciously or not) why the person doesn't put his or her name on the testimonial.

Key #1: A very specific claim

Don't use generalities like:
  "Great"
  "Awesome"
  "Wonderful"
  The more specific the claim, the more believable it is.

Key #2: An air of believability

It should be believable. NEVER, never make up testimonials. I'm okay with writing it for the person and asking them to give their OK if they agree with it, but don't just make them up.

Key #3: Benefit-packed claims

Make sure that each testimonial is full of benefits that your readers will receive by buying the book. So, don't say, "Great book!" Instead, say, "I learned how to find a new job for 25% more pay. I did it in less than 29 days too!" See the difference?

Key #4: Put their name on it

The most believable endorsements have the person's name on it, at the very least. It would be even better if you could get permission to use their city and if possible, their email. Now, this isn't always possible, but if you can get people to agree, your results will be dramatically better. The amount of credibility that is built with this kind of testimonial is incredible.

An example of a good (actual) book testimonial from one of our authors:

"Here is a powerhouse book of tips, tactics and approaches for earning extra income. A fantastic book."

— Jean-Guy Francoeur, author of Messy Manager

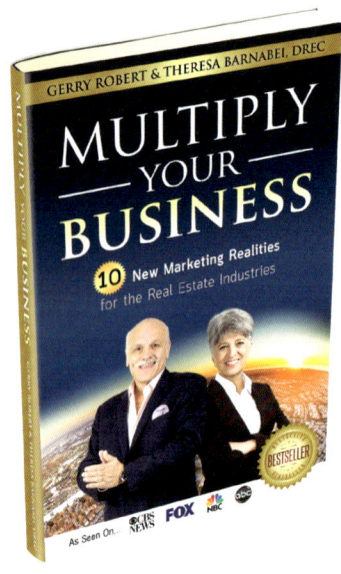

How to Get Testimonials

Here's how to get plenty of excellent testimonials:

Make a List

Make a list of everyone, I mean everyone who you might want to get an endorsement from. I remember for my first book, I wanted to get Tom Peters of the *In Search of Excellence* fame. He eventually turned me down, but that's okay, I got my second pick instead.

In writing this list, don't consider anything other than, "Would the readers of my book be influenced by this person or not?" If so, put them on the list. Find the contact info.

Depending on how famous and rich the person whom you want to write your foreword, endorsement or testimonial, it might be hard to actually get it into their hands. You might need a fair degree of patience and cunning persistence just to find their contact info. Use these things that other authors who have succeeded in getting testimonials have used:

- Directories

- Internet

- Guests of their show

Finding Celebrities

Many celebs use agents. You might want to consider asking their agent if they have a publicist, as sometimes it's easier to go through the publicist. They are interested in exposure for their clients. Agents are usually only interested in CASH.

Get the word out! (But draft the testimonial yourself!)

Too many people are too stingy to give away their books for FREE. However, giving away your book is often what you have to do to get testimonials. And the cost of doing this is a painless drop in the bucket compared with the firepower that good testimonials will bring to your sales copy.

Give away your book to some people and tell them why you're doing it. Tell them you want to get a testimonial about their experience with your book.

Tell them that you normally sell the book for X amount and the book will give them x, y, and z benefits. But you are willing to give it to them, for FREE, if they are willing to endorse you and the product.

Of course, you should be working on testimonials even before your book goes to press, so send them a few chapters on paper or maybe email them, or put the book in a diskette and mail it to them.

Write It Yourself!

I suggest that you actually write out the testimonial for them and tell them that you'd like to use it as is, or they are FREE to edit it if they prefer, assuming, of course, that they fully agree with the statement you wrote.

Most people will say yes. If you write it out for them, they won't have to, and that will make them more likely to say yes. Say something like this:

"Dear..., Would you consider endorsing my new book? I know you are busy. Considering your position and your schedule, I've written what I'm looking for in a testimonial for the enclosed book. In fact, after reading the book, if you agree with it, I can use it exactly as it is, or feel FREE to edit-at-will..."

Sample Letter

Dear Mr. Big-Time Celebrity,

I want to make you even more famous by including your prestigious name in my new book with a testimonial on Page 1 or the back cover. I know you are busy and I recognize that drafting an endorsement is a creative act – requiring time and thought.

So, I have come up with a suggested testimonial, one that ties into your background.

(INSERT CUSTOMIZED ENDORSEMENT HERE)

Feel FREE to edit-at-will or if after reading my book, you agree with it, we can use it as is.

As I am on a publisher deadline, I would appreciate your response by _____. (INSERT DATE)

Sincerely,

(INSERT YOUR NAME AND BOOK TITLE)

Additional Ideas

- Never have blank pages in the back of your book. Sell an ad, promote a charity or sell your product or service.

- Price your book on the high side of normal. Since most of my readers won't be selling many books in bookstores, the price is not so much of an issue. So make it high. You can always lower the price when you sell it live. The average hardcover book price in 2016 was about USD 36.00, while softcovers sold for USD 30.00.

- Include QR codes in your book. Just search online for FREE QR creators. One we use is qrstuff.com.

- Select a charity for your book. Call them up and tell them you've decided to donate a portion of book sales to them. Give them a chance to speak at your book launch gala and give them an ad for FREE at the back of your book. I play a four-minute video for my charity at every one of my bootcamps.

If you would like a **FREE** FUND IT™ Coaching Session with a Senior Publishing Consultant with Black Card Books, please send an email to cs@blackcardbooks.com.

PLAN IT
WRITE IT
PUBLISH IT
FUND IT
MOVE IT

Chapter Four

It's not uncommon for our authors to bring in $10,000, $20,000 even $30,000 or more before they write one single word using this FUND IT™ System.

4

FUND IT

Only Read This Chapter If You Want to Make Money Flow Directly to You Even before You Write a Single Word of Your Book.

- The CASH Concept.
- The Gerry Robert FUND IT™ System.
- Sell Books Using a Simple Little Buy Now Card™.
- See the System That Has Generated Millions of Dollars by Selling Ads in the Back of Books.
- One Tool (Feature Profile) That Will Bring in an Additional $6,000 to $10,000.
- How to Sell a BONUS Chapter for $7,500 to $10,000 to a JV Partner.
- Generate More Than $3,000 per Speech Using the FUND IT™ Speaking System.
- The Magic Formula That Helped Ann Lim Earn $5,100 in a 15-Minute Talk *(the Order Form Close)*.

I believe you can earn a small fortune before your book is completed and, in some cases, before it is even started. What I want to share with you now is how you can get others to pay for all of the costs associated with publishing your book.

I came up with these strategies to solve a problem in my business. I offer a very highly-priced publishing program. At the time, I charged a $60,000 consulting fee. I wanted to figure out a way to get more people to hire us. So I figured out that if I could get these people to raise the money from other people, then it would be a no-brainer for them to purchase my services… It worked like a charm. Within a few years, I sold almost $20,000,000 worth of contracts.

I get creative when there's money at stake! Especially that amount.

What follows are a few of the methods we now teach to all our clients. What's good about these strategies is that you do not have to be a superstar salesperson to raise $10,000, $20,000 or $50,000. You can do it in a matter of 8 to 16 weeks. If you do it the way our clients do, you can do this before even starting your book.

How Did This System Come to Be?

One day, a participant in our seminar wanted to join my publishing program. The price at that time was $37,000. A lot of money for anyone. He took a leap and we began to work on his book. His name was Rev. Larry Marshall, a semi-retired minister. He made money as an officiant at weddings. He wanted to write a book entitled *It's Your Wedding*. It was a great book to help people plan their weddings. It had wedding vows, sample speeches, checklists and it was very well-written.

He paid the required deposit to join my publishing program and about five months later, he called me to tell me he was going to have to drop out of the program because he just couldn't afford to continue. This saddened me. See, I like to get paid when people owe me money.

I asked him if he would consider staying with the program if I showed him how to raise the money. It took him a fraction of a second to answer. What I came up with almost 20 years ago was the beginnings of this FUND IT™ System.

So here's what we did: We made a list of companies who currently advertise to his readers – people who were getting married. Just think about who that might be. We came up with the following list:

- Wedding planners
- Limo companies
- Dressmakers
- Suit rental companies
- Wedding singers
- Caterers
- Insurance agents
- Florists

AUTHORS WANTED

Scan this QR code to send an email to
bonnie@blackcardbooks.com
and get more information on how I might partner with you on your book and have it published
by my publishing company, Black Card Books.

And he sold them all a full-page ad in the back of his book under a section entitled 'Resources the Author Recommends'. He raised tens of thousands before the book was even finished. You can too!

I figured that if we approached those people and offered them an opportunity to get a full-page ad in the back of the book, they would jump at the idea. They did!

That was the impetus of this system that has literally raised millions of dollars for our authors. I was questioned by a number of people on our executive team about why would I share this information in a book like this. They thought I was nuts, but I know that if it can help you get your book out, it's a good thing. Some of you will want to partner your book with me and will inquire about our publishing program. Even if you don't, what follows is a very powerful system for you to raise enough money to pay for all of the costs to publish your book.

Rev. Marshall approached vendors who wanted to get in front of people getting married and was, indeed, able to pay the remainder of his balance to me in short order.

The FUND IT™ System

First, we will discuss some foundational elements then delve deeper into six methods that you may want to use to fund your entire publishing project. This section is critical to your success – it's the heart of the system.

Preparation

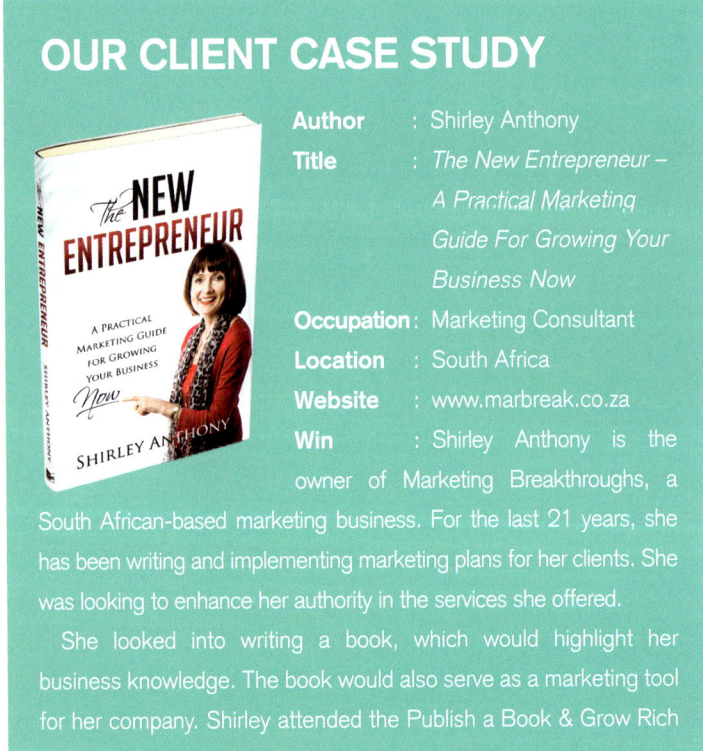

OUR CLIENT CASE STUDY

Author : Shirley Anthony
Title : *The New Entrepreneur – A Practical Marketing Guide For Growing Your Business Now*
Occupation : Marketing Consultant
Location : South Africa
Website : www.marbreak.co.za
Win : Shirley Anthony is the owner of Marketing Breakthroughs, a South African-based marketing business. For the last 21 years, she has been writing and implementing marketing plans for her clients. She was looking to enhance her authority in the services she offered.

She looked into writing a book, which would highlight her business knowledge. The book would also serve as a marketing tool for her company. Shirley attended the Publish a Book & Grow Rich bootcamp and discovered how to develop partnerships with other business owners that would, in turn, assist with the funding of her book.

Following The FUND IT™ system, as taught to her by Black Card Books, Shirley interviewed several successful business owners. She approached people by phone and email, and out of 53 attempts, she secured interviews with 50 professionals.

Over the span of a few months, she secured six business partnerships through these interviews that led to the funding of her book. Shirley clearly learned that the more contacts you make, the more opportunities for successful funding partnerships you will have.

Before she even finished writing her book, Shirley pre-sold 525 copies through The FUND IT™ system and interview campaign.

Now a published author, Shirley continues to use her book as a marketing tool, and she has created a network of amazing professionals, which she now uses to provide even greater services to her clients.

The basic idea is that you are going to sell to companies that don't compete with you but are complementary to your business. This provides them an opportunity to benefit from all of the publicity and promotion around your book. As an author, you now own a financial asset that you can trade upon. You have something very valuable that people will pay you to be associated with, provided you do it right. We have all kinds of people in our program who would never ever consider themselves salespeople but are enjoying huge financial success because the system is so powerful. If you just follow the system, you will be able to enjoy similar results.

The first thing you need to do is make a list of companies who currently advertize to your T.POP. Let's face it: Finding effective ways of advertising is more critical today than ever. A book, although a new medium, is a very prestigious place to advertise. Companies are always looking for unique advertising places that promise to put them in front of their target market.

For them, advertising costs are always on the increase and results on the decrease. When you approach them, they are very intrigued. Make a long list of companies that currently spend money to influence your readers.

Do not list big companies. We have strategies to approach big companies but that is only after you publish your book. For now, you want small companies who will give you money immediately. You want the cash now!

Big companies will need to see your book before they ever consider partnering with you. At this stage, as in right now, you don't likely have your book written. By the way, you don't need to have anything written other than your title, subtitle and table of contents. You will need something we call an Advertising Kit, which I will cover soon.

Another problem with big companies is that they move slowly. I want you to put cash in your pocket in a matter of days, not months. If you approach a big company, especially publicly traded companies, they will insist on passing your book through their legal department. That can take forever.

Attitude

You should have the attitude that you are giving small companies an opportunity to partner with you in a very unique and prestigious advertising vehicle. You are not begging them to give you money. You have an asset and you are trading on that asset. Besides, this is a very affordable vehicle for them to get their message out to prospects – your readers. If they currently advertise now to influence that group, they may be very interested in hearing about your offer. Still…

MOST WILL SAY NO – YOU HAVE TO DEAL WITH IT. When selling any product, most people will not take you up on your offer. You only need a few to say YES.

Interviews

Interviews are a very effective way for you to get great content for your book and (more importantly) set things in motion to sell them an advertisement in the back of your book.

with one multinational company who asked if she would be available to speak across the country for them. She conducted the interviews via Skype while working full time at her regular job. Needless to say, she doesn't work there anymore.

OUR CLIENT CASE STUDY

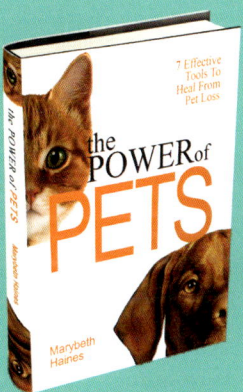

Author	: Marybeth Haines
Title	: *The Power of Pets – 7 Effective Tools To Heal From Pet Loss*
Occupation	: Pet Expert, Speaker and Coach
Location	: St. Catharines, Ontario, Canada
Website	: www.authormarybethhaines.com
Win	: Marybeth made a list of people who might want to advertise in a book about pets. She started calling them on the phone, requesting 20 minutes to interview them for her upcoming book. Out of the 89 calls she made, 82 people agreed to be interviewed for her book. This gave her enormous material for the book, but she also built rapport with these people – something that was crucial for her plan to sell them an ad. Marybeth was able to fund her entire book publishing program using this technique. She is also working on a speaking contract

Here are a few other suggestions for doing interviews:

- When you call to book the interview, never tell them your occupation. Telling them you are the author of an upcoming book is much more powerful.

- Limit the interview to 20 minutes.

- Before you leave, say this: "... My publisher has a way for you to benefit from all of the publicity and promotion that will happen when the book is released – is that something you might want to hear about at some point?" Who is going to say

NO to that? What you've done is open the door to talk about your advertising opportunity at some point in the future. When you go back to show them where you will be quoting them in your book, you remind them that they said they'd like to hear about how you can help them. You drop off an Advertising Kit (which I will show you later) and sell them a full-page ad at the back of your book if they agree to buy 100 books at retail.

Action

Now, you need to make a list of at least 100 people who currently advertise to your T.POP. Do this first: Make a list of 10 categories. If you are writing a book on weddings, ask yourself: What 10 categories of small companies would want to get in front of people who are getting married? The list could include limousine companies, florists, hotels, real estate agents and life insurance agents. Once you have the 10 categories, find the contact information for 10 companies in each category. Start with people you know. Maybe your real estate agent or your florist, if that is applicable. These are the people you approach first. Then fill the entire sheet with 10 companies in 10 categories. I'll show you a little later what to say and how to sell ads that will fund this entire project for you.

6 Money-Making Techniques That Will Bring in Money before You Write a Single Word

1. Buy Now Cards™

These small cards (11" x 2.83") are a small but very powerful way for you to sell books even before you write a single word. Why would anyone buy a book before it's even started? Because of the BONUS. I suggest offering something of greater value than your book to entice people to put an order in immediately. The card is perforated so you can keep the section on the right with their payment info, and they keep the section on the left with all your contact info and the bonus. This bonus needs to be low-cost to you, but with a highly perceived cost to them.

Some will buy it, some won't – so what? Do it anyway!!!

2. Sell Ads in the Back of Your Book for $3,400+

Here's the concept in a nutshell: You are going to do a chapter at the back of your book entitled Resources the Author Recommends. You can see my section on page 207. You will then sell full-page ads and place them here. This will make your book very practical and also give you a huge source of revenue. We've had people sell $50,000-$60,000 of ads in the back of their books.

In order to get an ad in your book, they should agree to buy 100 books.

The main document you need is what I call the Advertising Kit. You can download a sample by scanning this QR code. Study it and recreate one for yourself. Remember, you will have to speak to many people if you want to raise $30,000-$40,000 but you can do it. Also remember that MOST PEOPLE WILL SAY NO – do it anyway!

STOP CHASING NEW CLIENTS, GET MOBILIZED NOW!

MOBILIZE AND DISCOVER HOW MOBILE MARKETING CAN MAINTAIN A THRIVING BUSINESS AND SKYROCKET YOUR REVENUE!

All business owners think they have a 'lead generation problem', forever finding new ways to generate leads for your business. Just when you think you have it figured out, Google, Facebook or some other social media platform will change their algorithm and all your hard work is out the window. Make lead generation relevant by focusing on loyalty and repeat clients.

How?

Well to start with, here is a very rare opportunity to sit down with a modern-day marketing guru who can transform your business forever. A single strategy recommended by Malik Jaffer can rain down leads on your business and those leads will drive your sales for weeks, months, even years!

Register **NOW** for a **FREE** copy of *The Mobilizer*™ book at www.themobilizerguru.com/book-pabgr and automatically QUALIFY for a **FREE** *Mobilizer* Guru Consultation valued at $497.

Get this great book and talk to *The Mobilizer*™ Guru, Malik Jaffer, himself one-on-one to uncover the power of mobile marketing for your business. Register **NOW** for **FREE** here www.themobilizerguru.com/book-pabgr.

THE MOBILIZER

Phone number: +1 978 600 8398
Email address: malik@themobilizerguru.com
website: www.themobilizerguru.com

Use a professionally designed adkit to show your prospects you are a PLAYER!

Use any asset you have.

Use a strong author picture.

Design this as A4 size or 8.5" x 11".

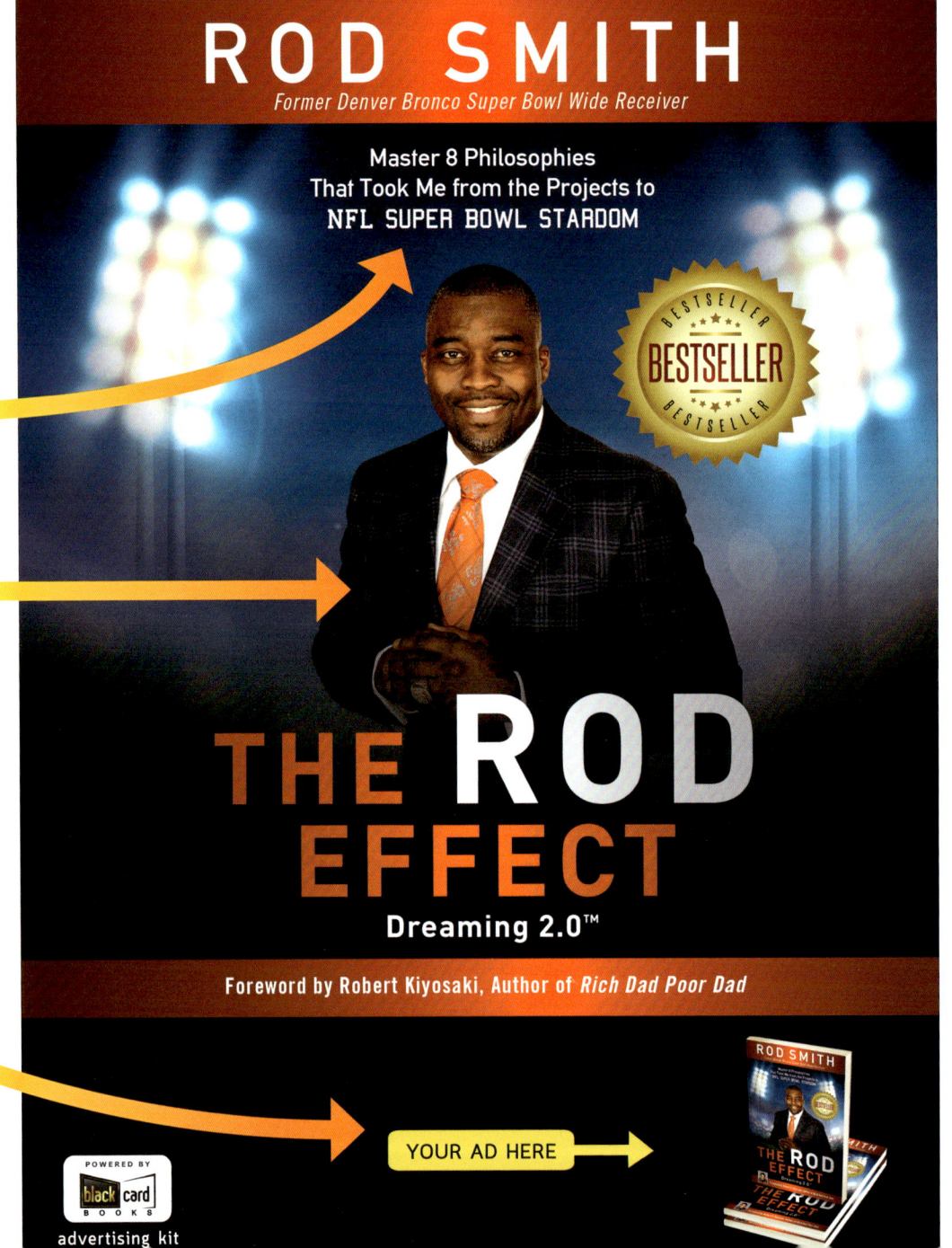

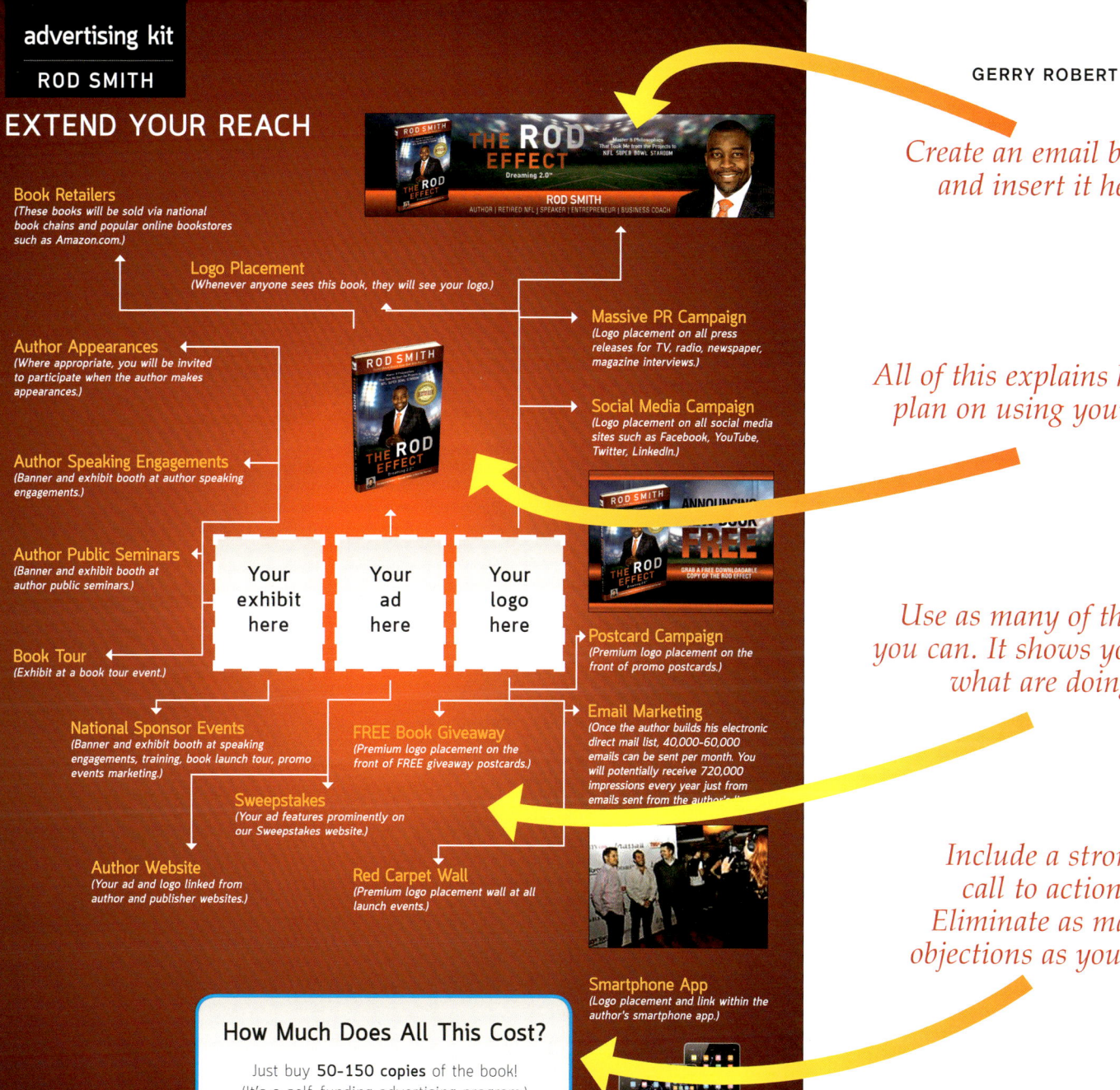

118 | FUND IT

THE BOOK

Describe your book in detail.

DESCRIPTION

Does today's economy have you feeling overworked, underpaid, and under appreciated?

Or are you like most feeling overqualified, time poor, and financially stressed?

Either way, you are looking for guidance, a blueprint, a playbook that's simple and easy to follow to help you dominate the future.

In this book, you will find eight Philosophies that wake you up and show you how dreaming can be manifested in all areas of your life.

Mr. Smith mastered eight philosophies that took him from welfare, food stamps and poverty into a multi-millionaire two-time Super Bowl Champion. After a stellar 14-year NFL career, he announced his retirement in 2008. Moving into private business, investing, and personal coaching he used the same principles to design the life he had always dreamed.

Now it's your time.

Learn to master these simple eight philosophies and turn your life around. These pages are filled with stories and example of how to get that done. The philosophies are simple and straightforward, so anyone can master them. What are you waiting on?

Start reading now, your future is waiting for you!

LEARN HOW...

- Can your finances use an upgrade? If you are limited in resources and still have big dreams, master the Law of Gratitude. It's a simple philosophy that will increase any amount of resources.

- If you are lost and have no idea how to get on the fast track of success, these pages will teach you to identify and master your burning desire to fulfill your life's purpose!

- Break the generational curse of poverty and lack in your family. Being responsible for your calling can be taught to the next generation through systematic actions that can be duplicated over a long period of time.

- Should your life have more success and significance? How are you going to fix it? Get a mentor! Read why your stubborn ways have halted your blessings. Get there faster with better guidance. Chapter 6 is perfect for you.

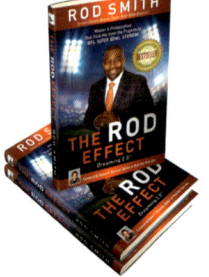

> "Give me 1 percent of your trust and I'll earn the other 99 percent."
>
> —ROD SMITH

advertising kit
ROD SMITH

THE BOOK

UNCOVER IN THESE PAGES...

The eight simple philosophies that took Rod Smith from the projects to NFL Super Bowl stardom. After he fully mastered these principles, he knew it was time to publish them for others to use. Too many people are lost; they lack guidance and a strong support system to help them achieve the life they desire and deserve. Included, you'll find stories of the real life struggles and successes Rod experienced, and perhaps in them, you'll discover answers you've been seeking to your own questions.

This playbook is simple, yet powerful.

They laughed when I said I had mastered eight philosophies of a seven-figure earner, but when my lifestyle changed, they begged me for my secret!

- Why I was chosen to show you a better way.
- What are you doing when no one is looking.
- Keeping the promises you made to yourself.
- Change your environment in two seconds.
- Death and life are in the power of the tongue.
- If you wouldn't trade places with someone, then don't take advice from them.
- The easiest things to do are not always best.
- Never be the smartest person in the room.
- What you are grateful for multiplies.
- Why not you.

> "Achieving success is not as hard as you think, but it's also not as easy as some people make it look."
>
> —ROD SMITH

Follow this design for maximum effect.

Remember, in marketing, so much of it is OPTICS! How you look. (Rod looks like a pro.)

120 | FUND IT

Write a detailed description of your readers.

Potential advertisers are spending money trying to influence this group.

REACH YOUR TARGET AUDIENCE

Advertise in a Published Book!

We are offering an opportunity for you to benefit from all of the publicity that will be generated when we launch this book and a way for you to advertise in the book itself, by putting your company directly in front of the readers of this book.

You've NEVER seen anything like this before! Advertising in the back of a book! You will be shocked about how little this costs compared to the numerous benefits.

We are doing a section at the back entitled, "Resources The Author Recommends", and you can place an ad for your company in the back of the book, be seen at every point when the book and/or author is promoted or publicized.

This is NOT for everyone. Dozens will apply, but we are only taking one (1) company per industry so if this interests you please contact us as soon as possible to see if your industry is still available.

If you want to position yourself and your organization in front of anyone looking for a playbook to guide them through physical, mental, financial, or emotional setbacks that have disrupted their life, then this proposal will be very exciting to you.

CONNECT

WITH ANYONE LOOKING FOR A PLAYBOOK TO GUIDE THEM THROUGH PHYSICAL, MENTAL, FINANCIAL, OR EMOTIONAL SETBACKS THAT HAVE DISRUPTED THEIR LIFE.

"Set your standards high and life will arrange itself to meet them."

—ROD SMITH

Insert your book cover here.

ADVERTISE IN HERE

Advertising Kit 5

advertising kit
ROD SMITH

RATE CARD

	BRONZE Buy 50 Books	SILVER Buy 75 Books	GOLD Buy 100 Books	PREMIERE Buy 150 Books
Full-Page Advert Placement for the Lifetime of the Book	✓	✓	✓	✓
Banner and Exhibit Booth at Book Launch Gala	✓	✓	✓	✓
Link on Campaign Website	✓	✓	✓	✓
Marketing Materials Co-Branding (Logo Placement)	✓	✓	✓	✓
Inclusion in Ongoing Social Media Campaigns	✓	✓	✓	✓
Link Placement in Promotional Email Marketing		✓	✓	✓
Industry Exclusivity		✓	✓	✓
Banner and Exhibit Booth at Public Speaking Events			✓	✓
Banner and Exhibit Booth at Author Public Appearances			✓	✓
Be Interviewed by Author and have Comments Included in the Book			✓	✓
Product Placement within Book			✓	✓
Logo Placement in TV/Radio/Magazine/Newspaper Press Releases			✓	✓
Logo Placement and Link within Smartphone App				✓
Author Endorsement from Stage				✓
1-Hour Author Keynote Speech/Workshop (Value USD 7,500)				✓
Investment	Buy 50 Books (USD 1,950)	Buy 75 Books (USD 2,925)	Buy 100 Books (USD 3,900)	Buy 150 Books (USD 5,850)

Inquire about the "Feature Profile" and/or "Chapter Contribution."

Offer 4 packages.

Price this in terms of book sales. They will receive a certain number of books. They can sell those books and thereby recoup all of their money. This then becomes a SELF-FUNDING marketing campaign.

122 | FUND IT

You can't show your book covers enough.

Include an order form for ease of payment.

THE ROD EFFECT
Dreaming 2.0™

Master 8 Philosophies That Took Me from the Projects to NFL Super Bowl Stardom

advertising kit
ROD SMITH

BOOK ORDER FORM
ROD SMITH
Author | Retired NFL Speaker | Entrepreneur | Business Coach

BUSINESS INFORMATION

Name
Address
City   Suite/Apt #
Prov/State   Country
Telephone   Postal / Zip Code
Fax
Email Address

PARTNERSHIP PACKAGES

Bronze USD 1,950   Silver USD 2,925   Gold USD 3,900   Premiere USD 5,850

Price   Tax   Total

PAYMENT DETAILS

EFT   Check   Visa   MasterCard   American Express   Other

Name on Card
Credit Card #   CVV
Expiry Date   /
Signature   Today's Date   /   /

- I agree to supply print-ready black and white artwork for my advert.
- I will receive all of the benefits listed on the previous page for the level I select. This also INCLUDES _____ FREE books which I can sell and keep all the money without royalty to the author.
- I authorize Rod Smith to debit my credit card for the option selected above.

Signature   Today's Date   /   /

Advertising Kit 7

advertising kit

ROD SMITH

THE AUTHOR

Rod Smith is an American Football Legend. He played 14 years in the NFL and retired with all the records for a non-drafted player. Just like his football career, Mr. Smith had to fight, claw, and scratch his way from the projects in Texarkana, Arkansas to the become a two-time Super Bowl Champion and soon to be in the Hall of Fame. He is a highly sought-after spokesman for several Fortune 500 companies like the Denver Broncos, FedEx, Visa, Cadillac, Nike, and Intuit to name a few. He earned three college degrees in business.

Growing up poor was a very humbling experience for Mr. Smith. As he climbed out of the ghetto to get full scholarships to college, he documented the process along the way.

Transitioning out of college to the NFL was no easy feat. But the same dreaming philosophies he used before would help propel him once again.

He studied and learned to master these eight simple, yet powerful philosophies that made him a multiple seven-figure earner. Along the path to success were some trials, some pain, and plenty of disappointments. All the while he crafted a playbook for a lifetime of success.

Since his retirement, he became an entrepreneur, real estate developer, and business coach. He used his success principles to build a multiple seven-figure real estate portfolio, over $50 million dollars in coffee revenue and has coached multiple families to seven-figure incomes.

Understanding how difficult it was to navigate through some of the troubled times, he decided to publish his playbook. Mr. Smith is known throughout the country as one of the hardest workers ever in his field. He will show you how the right playbook can have your success come from smart work, not hard work.

Write a strong author bio.

124 | FUND IT

advertising kit
ROD SMITH

BOOK INFO

As you get sponsors, insert their logos here.

Book Title:	The Rod Effect
Subtitle:	Master 8 Philosophies That Took Me from the Projects to NFL SUPER BOWL STARDOM
Price:	USD 39.00
ISBN:	978-1-77204-254-2
Phone Number:	+1 720 432 8009
Email Address:	rod@therodeffect.com
	support@therodeffect.com
Website:	www.therodeffect.com

POWERED BY

Publisher

Black Card Books

Suite 214
5-18 Ringwood Drive
Stouffville, Ontario
Canada L4A 0N2
Tel: +1 877 280 8536

www.blackcardbooks.com

Do not use the Black Card Books logo without written permission.

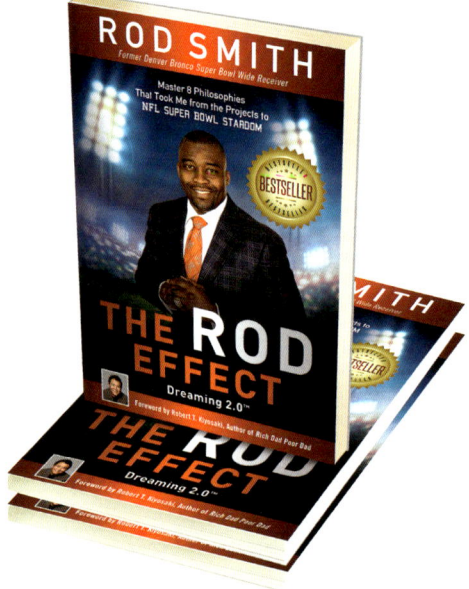

GERRY ROBERT | 125

Books Published by Black Card Books and Results
(Small Sample!)

THE WALL STREET JOURNAL.
www.wsj.com/articles/a-faux-pas-recovery-plan-1450821565

www.themoneykeys.com/media
Speaks to thousands via national speaking at conferences.

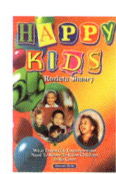

Author offered the book for FREE in newspaper ads.

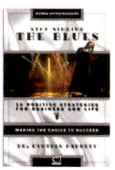 

www.refiredontretire.com
Author appeared in *Time* Magazine and other national media outlets.

The Washington Post

Author uses the book to book speaking engagements for national conferences.

These are additional benefits of publishing your book with Black Card Books.

We get RESULTS!

I will publish your book.

Send an email to cs@blackcardbooks.com and request for an interview with one of our publishing consultants.

GERRY ROBERT | 127

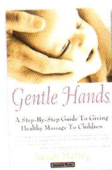 

gentlehandsbook.com

Susan Harley packages her book with products and sells it in gift and maternity shops throughout Australia.

www.karinhagberg.com

Karin uses the book to get publicity and also to attract customers.

Uses his book to speak at home shows throughout Australia.

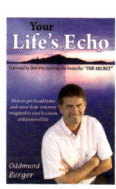 

Oddmund Berger uses the book to get publicity. He also gives his book using our "My Mentor" technique.

Used his book to recruit a sales team of over 10,000.

Advertising in a book makes so much sense because...

It's an ad but it doesn't feel like an ad.

When people are reading a book they are in an educational mode; their minds are wide open.

Authors are perceived as trusted experts. Their endorsement is powerful for you.

The promotional possibilities around a book are limitless.

A book is the key to open the door to publicity on radio, TV, newspapers, magazines.

You get instant differentiation.

Books are never thrown out. Your ad will have longevity.

Authors are invited to speak to large groups.

3. Sell Feature Profiles for $5,000+

A Feature Profile is a bigger ad, which might be inserted throughout the book. It allows your advertiser a chance to explain their story or message, they could provide some tips or strategies to help your readers and it, of course, gives their contact details. If they are smart, they will also offer something for FREE… I call that magnet an AMD or AME (Attraction Marketing Device or Event). You could also make this a *Case Study* or a *Best Practice* type of profile. You don't want many of these, say three or four max. This could be offered as a huge bonus if they buy your Premiere Package. Price suggestions are in the Advertising Kit.

See pages 60-61 and 130-131 for Feature Profiles I got for this book. These people really can help you.

FEATURE PROFILE

Sarah Jones
Real Estate Agent

MY FAVORITE QUOTE

❝ Dress for success. Image is very important. People judge you by the way you look on the outside ❞
Brian Tracy

DRESS FOR SUCCESS
Sassy Tips for a Success Breakthrough

If you want to look successful & make a great first impression do a check up from the neck up and back down again!

1. How is your hair? Has anyone said lately, I love the color! What a great cut! Your hair looks awesome! If not, go to the best colorist, the best stylist you can find and GET IT DONE!!!

2. What is the look of your best business suit? Is it out dated? Is it cheap (I don't mean what you paid for it; I mean fabric, style....) Does it fit? Is the hem right for your leg? Is the color the best for you? You are making a statement... what is it?

3. Shoes...what are you wearing? Are they cheap? Do they look cheap? Are they a comfortable heel? Attractive heel? Nice leather? Good tip (not click clack...I used to call those my fall in the mall shoes! ha!)

4. Hose..... are they beautiful and look special on your leg? Never wearing black hose with white or red shoes!

5. Make up.... who is especially good with the product in your area? Ask for advice or a makeover..... Are you still wearing the same shades in the same places you were a year ago? Lip stick? Same? Liners? Same? Make sure you look your absolute best!!!!

6. Personal...have you had your teeth cleaned recently? I mean it! Go to the dentist and get that plaque off! What do your fingernails and toenails look like? How is your breath? And what breath mint do you carry with you?

7. What does your ink pen look like?

8. Brief case or folio?

9. What does your purse look like? Is it cheap? Too big? Too small?

10. What are your business cards being carried in? Make sure not "tattered". How accessible are they?

11. Are your earrings outdated? Cheap? Too big? Other jewelry? Too much, too little? Go for classic!

12. Do your clothes fit? Do you need to have a jacket taken up, skirt up or down, sleeves raised?

13. Are your leather articles polished? (Shoes, purse, etc...)

SARAH's STORY

"I want to stand for what is positive in life for women because when you change the life of a woman, you not only change her family, you change the life of the world."

Changing lives. School president from first grade through college and Head of her Class Independent National Sales Director Your name here loves to lead women. "It was, in fact, while attending a private women's college, that I developed a passion for issues that appeal to women," Your name here explains.

Single and an only child, Your name here proudly describes the women she knows through her Mary Kay business as extended family and incredible mentors. "My Independent Executive National Sales Director Emeritus taught me to have 'big-girl' dreams, my Executive NSD Emeritus taught me to love people to success, my Senior National Sales Director taught me how to work strategically, while my Elite Executive National Sales Director taught me how to live with passion. They changed my life; I love passing it on!"

Your name here favorite memory happened during a private meeting with the founder of the company in her office. "I will never forget her 'velvet' hands holding mine as she said, 'I want you to become one of my National Sales Director daughters.'"

Likewise, Your name here appreciates the strong support of both her parents. "Mom is one of my top Independent Sales Directors and a future offspring NSD, and my dad is one of my biggest fans who has been inspired to assist me in my office."

Your name here enthusiastically encourages the wonderful women of her National area to run to the finish line with their tongue hanging out. "I want to stand for what is possible in life for women because when you change the life of a woman, you change the life of the world!"

CONTACT

SARAH JONES
REAL ESTATE AGENT

Suite 214 5-18 Ringwood Drive
STOUFFVILLE, Ontario
CANADA, L4A 0N2
Phone: +1 (877) 280 8536

FREE VIDEO
"How to Prepare Your Home For Sale."

CALL
+1 (877) 280 8536

or email
myfreereport@info.com
TODAY!

FEATURE PROFILE
Stephen McCullagh

"SMEs are the heart and soul of the economy." Small and Medium-Sized Enterprises (SMEs) create more jobs locally and recycle a much larger share of their revenue back into their local economies than chain and online stores. SMEs are finding it harder to survive – they need to learn how to fight back.

Stephen has over 20 years of IT experience both in the corporate world and as a small business owner. In that time, he has spent time coaching and supporting SMEs in many different sectors.

Customer loyalty counts. It costs 5 to 7 times more money to attract a new customer than to retain an existing customer.

With the valuable insights and observations gained while dealing with SMEs, Stephen founded the Local Small & Medium Enterprise Alliance (LSMEA). The LSMEA creates groups of local SMEs connected to support each other. The message is clear: Supporting local businesses is vital to the life of their local economy, and for the survival of their villages, towns, and cities.

"We cannot solve our problems with the same thinking we used when we created them."

ALBERT EINSTEIN

"A business has to be involving, it has to be fun, and it has to exercise your creative instincts."

SIR RICHARD BRANSON

LOYALTY PAYS
10 TIPS TO KEEP YOUR CUSTOMERS COMING BACK

1. Staff loyalty counts. Businesses with high customer loyalty also have high staff loyalty. Customers build relationships with staff members. If your staff changes, the relationships formed have to be built again.

2. The 80/20 Rule. Eighty percent of most business's revenue comes from 20% of their customers. Know who these customers are, connect with and reward these customers for their loyalty.

3. Stages of loyalty. Customers that become loyal to a company go through 6 stages. Suspect, Prospect, Initial Customer, Repeat Customer, Client and Advocate. Know what stage your customer is at and treat them accordingly.

4. Serve then sell. Customers today are more informed, smarter, and less tolerant of being "sold to". Where they experience great customer service elsewhere, they expect it with your business. Being personalised, productive and pleasant is now expected; if you don't deliver, they will leave.

5. Pursue customer complaints. Only 10% of customer complaints arise, the other 90% go unreported and can lead to many undesired responses such as bitterness towards staff, unpaid invoices and most damaging – unfavourable word of mouth advertising.

6. Be responsive. Research shows that from a customer's point of view, responsiveness and customer service go hand in hand. Customers are now expecting rapid responses from customer care.

7. Know your customers' interpretation of value. The key to your customers' loyalty is "value"; knowing how your customers interpret that value is crucial to building solid customer loyalty. Survey your customers for valuable insights.

8. Don't hide behind technology. Ensure that there is a route to a human behind your electronic communications. Your customer is less likely to do business if it's difficult to speak to someone.

9. Define and unify customer service. Whether it's a physical high street store, an online store or a phone line, all store fronts must be uniform in their approach to customer service. Customers now expect to be able to move from one store to another with the same excellent level of service.

10. Data is an asset. Collecting and analysing data is paramount to understanding who your best and worst customers are. Knowing when a customer has been absent from your business for a period allows you to contact that customer and offer incentives to "come back". Obtaining customer details allow the creation of electronic newsletters and customer surveys to keep in touch with your customer base.

For a **FREE** membership of the LSMEA and suggestions for implementing these 10 tips exclusive to readers of Gerry Robert's *Publish a Book & Grow Rich*, go to:
www.lsmea.com/pabgr

4. Sell One Bonus Chapter for $10,000+

This is a great idea and you only sell one of these. It might sell for $7,500 to $10,000. This is where you allow a sponsor the opportunity to submit a chapter called a BONUS CHAPTER for inclusion in your book. The benefits for them are enormous: They get their information in your book for the life of that book. They can even get FREE publicity if they send a well-written press release to the media.

I practice what I preach. Turn to page 197 to read Ed Nq's Bonus Chapter for this book. It's entitled DIGITAL EMPIRE HACK. It's rich with content and practical advice.

OUR CLIENT CASE STUDY

Author : Jean Ann Dorrell
Title : *Don't Be A Victim! Protect Yourself– Everything Seniors Need To Know To Avoid Being Taken Financially*
Occupation : Certified Estate Planner
Location : Florida, USA
Website : www.jeananndorrell.com
Win : I suggested this idea to Jean Ann and she loved it. She asked me how much to charge and since the idea was new to me, I blurted out $10,000. She called me a few weeks later telling me that she had some good news and some bad. The good news was that she had sold a bonus chapter to a law firm. The bad news was that she didn't get $10,000, she was only able to get $7,500. Wow!!! Seven thousand, five hundred dollars to a law firm is nothing.

Get the company to submit a chapter that is 2,000 to 3,000 words long. It must be real content offering great strategies. It can't be a brochure on why they are so great. It really needs to add to the content of the book. It needs to be informational, not commercial.

5. Sell Speeches for $3,400+

Here's a novel idea for selling speeches: Let's say you are writing a book entitled *8 Ways to Boost Your Child's Self-Esteem*. You make a list of private schools in your area. Send them all a letter offering to put on an event that will serve three purposes:

- It's a marketing event for their school.

- It's a customer appreciation event for their current customers.

- It's a fund-raiser for the school's favourite charity.

You tell them that you will forgo your speaking fee if they would simply agree to buy 100 copies of your book at retail, and that you would even help them sell those books at the event.

This event will be an evening seminar and features you, the author of a new book. You provide them with tickets, brochures and envelopes with a letter inside. To the school's prospects, people who might have inquired about the school, you send two tickets to the event (make sure you have a price on the tickets of $29 each), a brochure and a letter. The school letter simply says that you had checked out their school at some point in the past and that you must care about children, and that you were sponsoring this event and wanted to give them two FREE tickets.

To existing students, you give two tickets to each child. Tell them it's simply a way for you to say THANK YOU for being a customer. Then you contact the school's charity and tell them they can come to the evening seminar and a portion of all of the books sold that night will go to the charity.

In order for this to work, you need to do most of the work because if the school senses that this will mean lots of work for them, they will be less likely to say yes.

Everyone wins with this technique.

The audience wins because they get a great lecture on a subject dear to their hearts for FREE.

The school wins because they get marketing, customer appreciation and a fund-raising event in one, and it won't cost them a penny because hopefully you can sell the 100 books they buy at the event.

You win because you've just sold 100 books at retail.

6. Use the Order Form Close to Bring in Thousands of Dollars

A True Story

One of our graduates is Anne Lim from Malaysia, the author of *Mad Dogs and Crazy Cats*. One day she came running up to me and gave me a big hug. She was estatic! "Gerry, you wouldn't believe what happened last night," she exclaimed. I was very intrigued. She continued, "I earned $5,100 last night." WOW!

She explained she had attended a large networking meeting and had used our ORDER FORM CLOSE. She said, "I just followed all of the steps and it was incredible." Anne learned to be prepared and she simply followed the steps I outlined for her.

"Gerry, 171 people bought my book... Right on the spot!"

The beauty of what Anne shared was that the most she had ever earned in a single month was $3,600. Then she earned $5,100 in a single night.

I was overjoyed. "How's the book coming along, Anne?" I asked. She put her head down. "Haven't even started yet!"

Of course, if you take money from someone for a book, you have to deliver the book.

Here's what happened: Anne was going to a huge women's networking event. When they found out that she was the author of an upcoming book, they asked her to speak for 10-15 minutes on her book. Since she had her book cover picture with her, they popped it onto a PowerPoint slide. Following my advice, she had order forms placed on each seat, one for everyone at the conference, about 800 women.

They introduced her as the author of the upcoming book *Mad Dogs and Crazy Cats – How Men Are Like Dogs and Women Like Cats*. She gave her quick lecture and, at the end, offered an incredible bonus if they agreed to buy the book that night. I can't remember what that bonus was, it doesn't matter – what matters is that it needs to be low-cost to you and a high perceived cost to the customer. The bonus needs to be more valuable than the book itself. That's why they will give you money before you write a single word. One hundred seventy-one people bought that book.

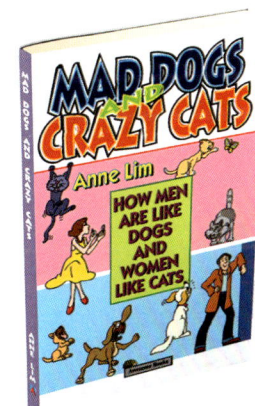

These Black Card Books authors attended my Publish a Book & Grow Rich bootcamp:

GET YOUR FREE* TICKET HERE

www.publishabookandgrowrich.com/freeticket

*Not applicable in every country.

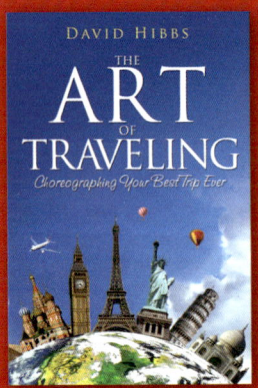

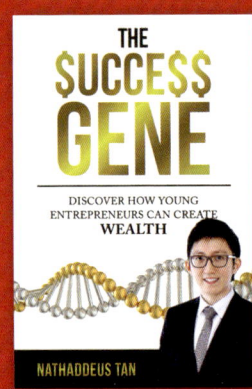

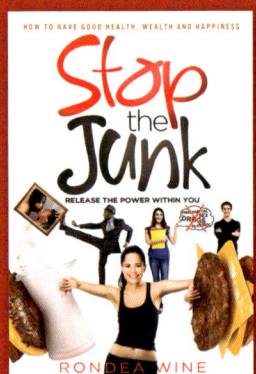

Chapter Five

PLAN IT
WRITE IT
PUBLISH IT
FUND IT
MOVE IT

GETTING the book is the easy part.

GETTING RID of the book,
now that's the challenge.

5

MOVE IT

What to Do with Your Book That Will Bring in More Prospects than You Know What to Do with and Cause the CASH to FLOW in Your Direction.

- Why Your Marketing Sucks and How a Book Can Make You a National Hero.
- The Campaigns That Work EVERY TIME for EVERYONE to Sell Books by the Truckload.
- MOVE IT – What to Do with Your Book That Will Bring in More Prospects than You Know What to Do with.

The Beeping of the Reversing Truck

Like most of you, for years I had focused only on 'getting' the book, what to write about, where I would find the time, what I would put into the book. The whole focus was on getting that book published. In my case, I had to borrow the money to pay for the printing. In the '80s, in order to get a good unit price, you had to order 5,000 books or more. It's no longer the case, but it was then. I took out a second mortgage on my little townhouse to get those books.

Finally, the big truck backs up into my tiny driveway and beep, beep, beep, beep is what I hear. The driver flings open the back door of this truck and it hit me like a tonne of bricks. Do you have any idea what 5,000 books look like? It filled most of my single-car garage. That was the very first time that I had given any thought to WHAT THE HELL AM I GOING TO DO WITH THESE BOOKS?

"It's 90% marketing and 10% content!"

— Jack Canfield, co-creator of the *Chicken Soup* series. Sold 500,000,000 books. Jack knows what he's talking about.

I quickly found out that...

> **It's called a BESTSELLING book, not BEST-WRITTEN book for a reason.**

That was the first time I had ever thought about what to do with those books. I got busy trying to answer that question – and I haven't stopped asking that question!

It was a major mindset shift for me.

Now the work begins!

A big mistake that authors make is thinking that their book will sell itself. It's not enough anymore to just write a good book. You also have to promote it.

Selling in Bookstores Is Dumb!

Yes, I said it. Do you have any idea how hard it is to get your books in bookshops? It's tough, trust me. Then if you are lucky enough to get them in there, they better sell like hotcakes in the first six to eight weeks or it'll be off the shelf in a heartbeat because there are 5,000 more books coming down the pike.

Also, I'm all about finding the BIGGEST CASH. And why would you chase $5-$10 selling a book when you could use that same book to bring in thousands?

Selling Books on Amazon.com and Other Big Retailers

The only reason I recommend putting your book on the big retailers like Amazon.com is the credibility it gives you and that's about it. If you tell someone you are an author, the first thing they are going to do is go to Amazon.com and see if your book is listed there. But the idea of getting rich selling books with online retailers is a myth (for most people). Can you hit a homerun and make millions? Sure. People point to my two good friends, Jack Canfield and Mark Victor Hansen, from the *Chicken Soup for the Soul* fame! They've done pretty good in bookshops and online. Sure, they have.

They have sold 500 million copies of those books. But really, what's the likelihood of that happening to you or me? You would have more luck winning the lotto and getting hit three times by lightning than selling 500 million books.

Instead, go after THE SURE THING. What is that?

Use your book as a marketing tool for your business and mitigate against the shift in consumer mindset towards any of use who sell anything. Just think about it, today, like never before in history, prospects are…

- Skeptical of those of us who sell things.

- They are distrustful of marketing efforts.

- They are overwhelmed with marketing messages – up to 5,000 per day.

- They shut us out.

- They don't want to be sold to.

- They think all marketers are liars.

So my recommendation is that you use your book to bring in huge revenues by having the book solve all of these barriers that consumers put up when anyone tries to sell to them.

The Reticular Activation System (RAS)

There is a small pea-shaped part of our brain called the Reticular Activation System (RAS). Its function is to filter out non-essential bits of data. For example, look around you right now: Look how many facts you are currently filtering out. That is, you are not conscisouly thinking about all of those points until I bring them to your attention. What's keeping you from thinking of all of those bits of information is the RAS.

As a marketer, you need to understand that today, that filter is 100 times thicker than ever before. Consumers instantly put up a huge barrier whenever they feel like someone is trying to sell them something. They resist all marketing messages today. But there is one tool that instantly, effortlessly and consistently penetrates that filter and garners you and your message a place in the mind of prospects. What is that tool? Your book.

There isn't a tool on the planet that has the power to disarm skeptical, distrusting people like a book can. Nothing opens doors like a book. There isn't an easier way to INSTANTLY change the way people look at you like your own book can. And that tool is the single best income-boosting tool there is.

Penetrate the consumer filter every single time. It's easy!

There is so much marketing noise out there and if you want to be heard in today's marketplace, you need something called CONTENT MARKETING.

> You can overcome a person's skepticism by showing how you can improve his life.

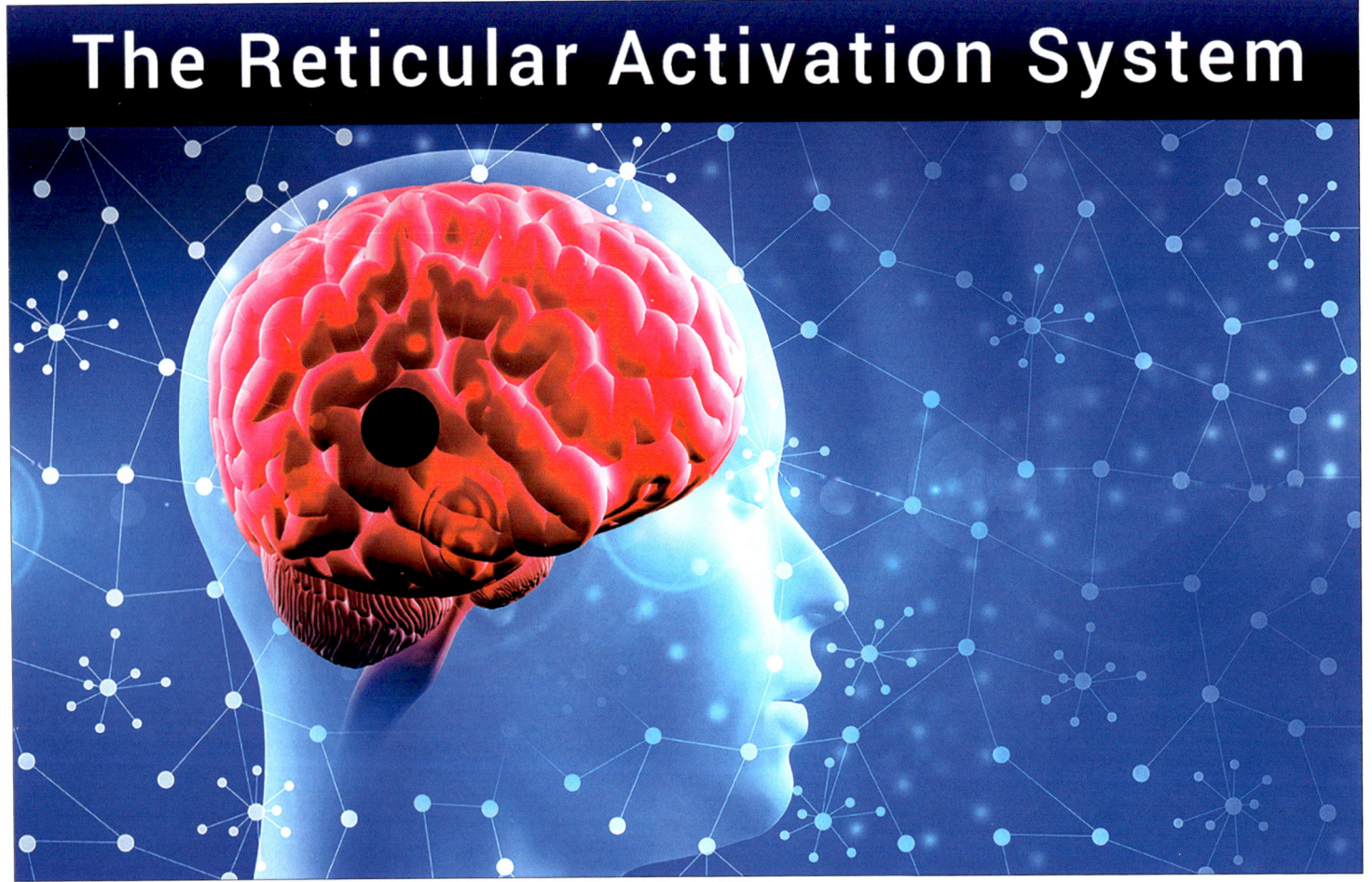

Your prospects have problems and are seeking solutions. If you give them those solutions, as an author, you will eliminate all other hurdles your competition has to contend with and thereby attract more prospects, make more sales and catapult your income.

People today are looking to avoid PAIN and they are looking for GAIN. So, the way to win them over is to solve something that they are looking to move away from (PAIN) or to obtain something they are seeking to move toward (GAIN).

Let's say you are in a restaurant and someone yelled, "There's a guy in the lobby shooting people!" (PAIN) What would everybody do? Get the heck out of there, right? No matter what they were thinking about two seconds before, the minute they feel threatened, they become conscious of nothing else. If you want to market to these people, show them how to avoid PAIN. That instantly gets you into their heads.

Let me ask you… How long would it take for you to grab your iPhone and record a three-minute video giving people five or six simple strategies to help them solve some problem you know they have? Most people I ask that question to in my seminars say it would take them less than an hour.

And if I asked you to put a simple statement at the end of the video that offered them a FREE downloadble version of your book and all they had to do was go to your landing page or opt-in page, you could do that, right?

If someone listens to a three-minute video, then clicks on a link to get your FREE book, you've just found yourself a REAL HOT prospect. Now, go sell them.

The Money Is in the Database

I'm sure you agree that you could do a three-minute video like that right now. Right?

"Content marketing is using content that you create to attract people so that they will become part of your sales process."

— Joanna Penn, author of *How to Market a Book*

Then I would suggest you put it up on www.YouTube.com; you wouldn't have any problem doing that, right? Of course not.

The thing you need to remember is that your prospects are searching right now for answers to their needs, desires and problems. Where do they search? The Internet, of course. So, if that one three-minute video that you just uploaded on YouTube catches their attention, you might have just found yourself a hot prospect. Now, here's where it gets really fun.

Let's say you took that one video and uploaded it on a video submission website like www.waach.com or any other VIDEO SUBMISSION website. They will upload your video to 20 or more sites just like www.YouTube.com. And its FREE! They do have paid plans as well, giving you many additional features.

Now, this one three-minute video that would take you less than an hour to do could be uploaded to more than 20 other sites. Now you have 21 fishing lines, as it were, in the river where your propects are swimming looking for answers.

Now, could you take that same three-minute video and create a small PowerPoint slideshow to accompany it? Sure, you could. Well, if you took that slideshow and uploaded it on www.slideshare.net, you could be exposing that video to tons more prospects who go to that website every day seeking solutions to their pain. Last month, they had 51,000,000 unique visitors.

Can you see how you are increasing your reach now and all you've done is film a three-minute video helping your prospects avoid pain or showing them how to gain? And you agreed that that video would take you less than an hour to produce.

Now imagine you stripped away the video – you'd be left with just the audio. It would most likely be in mp3 format. That's also known as a podcast. Do you have any idea how many places are looking to distribute good podcasts? You might have heard of one of them… iTunes.

There are millions upon millions of people seeking help and their preferred methods to consuming that content is via audio. There are tons of people like me with databases in the hundreds of thousands and even millions of followers on Facebook or Twitter who are willing to share your podcast with our lists – assuming you have good solid 'meat' for our listeners.

Now how many fishing lines do you have in the river? And all from one single three-minute video. What if you did one a day? Even one per week! Heck, even one per month?

Now, people no longer see you as a salesperson; they see you as a trusted advisor. Someone they can trust. And if you want to make money in today's hostile marketplace… better gain their trust!

Nothing Garners Trust Like Your Own Published Book!

In our bootcamps, we spend all of the last day just helping people MOVE IT. You can have a good book, but if you can't get rid of them, it'll do you nor anyone else any good. What follows are some of the most popular campaigns from that seminar.

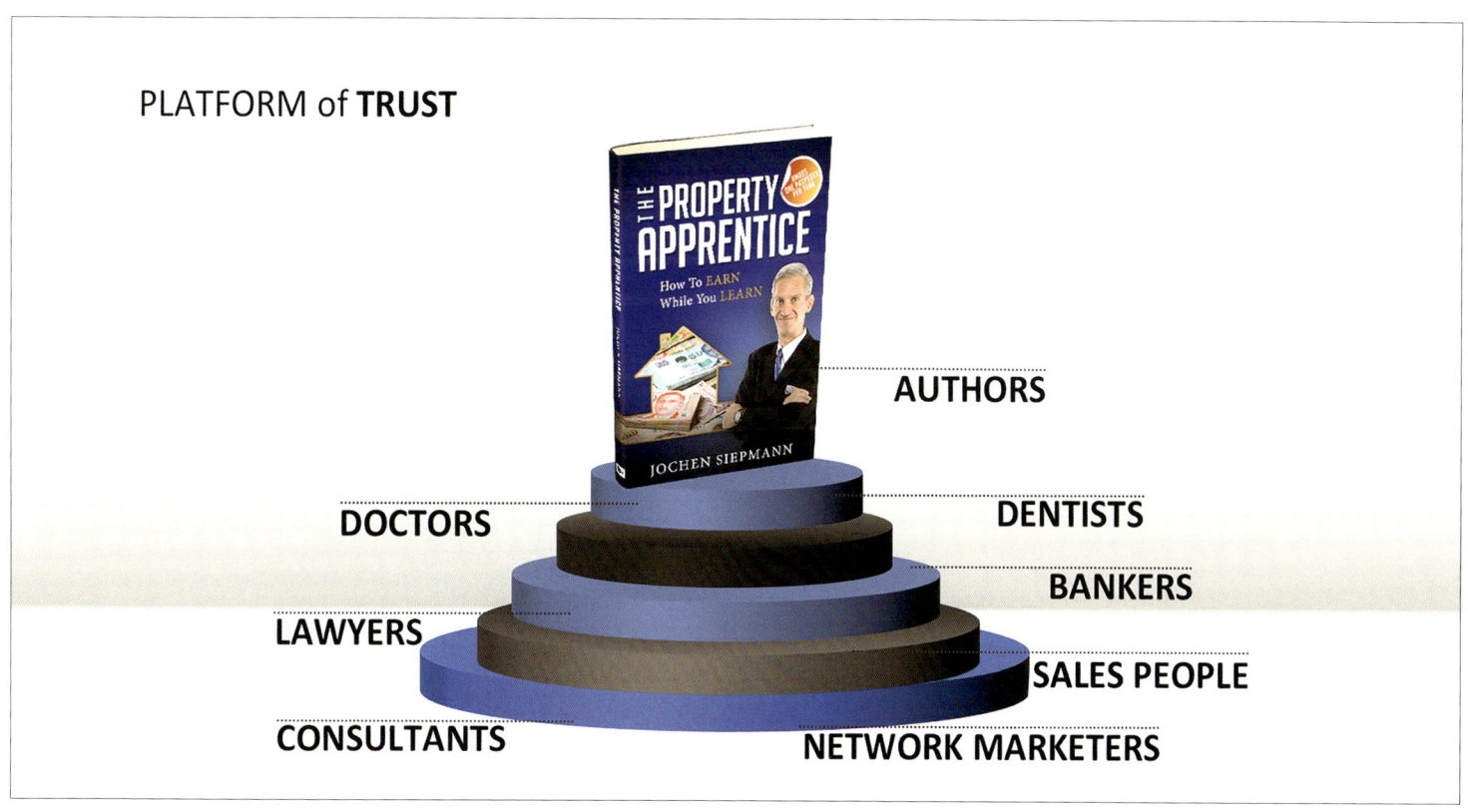

MAJOR CAMPAIGN: The Author Announcement Campaign

Campaign Objective: To get publicity right now, even before you write a single word.

Are you aware that you can get FREE publicity simply by announcing that you are publishing a book? You can, and it's easy.

I live in a small town just north of Toronto, Canada. We have five or six pharmacies. One day, I was flipping through my small community newspaper and saw this article about one of the pharmacists writing a book.

Just the fact that you have a book coming out soon is newsworthy.

You might not think it is, but trust me, it is of interest and the media will give you coverage if you follow the steps below.

This article appeared in my hometown newspaper announcing his upcoming book.

The Stouffville Sun, Tuesday, March 4, 2003, page 5

Main St. pharmacist has right prescription in book

By Hannelore Volpe
Stouffville Sun

Shortly after Stouffville pharmacist Farid Wassef's book "Breaking the Age Barrier" was released last month, he took his strategies for healthier aging to TV audiences.

He was a guest last week on CHTV's "Body and Health" program on channel 11 and on Global TV's evening news talking about his ideas on staying healthy and active even late in life. He'll soon be travelling across Canada to promote the book and talk about his ideas on complementary therapies and medicines.

More than 3,000 copies of the book flew off the shelves of major Canadian book stores within two weeks of its release.

In the book, subtitled "Strategies for Optimum Health, Energy and Longevity", Mr. Wassef has distilled the knowledge he's gained in his 15 years as a pharmacist at Houston Pharmacy on Stouffville's Main Street and his 20 years of research into the roles of lifestyle, stress reduction, nutrition and alternative medicines and therapies on increasing well-being and health.

The book is co-authored by fellow pharmacist Sherry Torkos, who practices holistic pharmacy in the Niagara Region.

Mr. Wassef believes since diseases aren't triggered by just one factor, successful treatment has to be multi-dimensional too, integrating both traditional and complementary therapies.

Stress, diet, environmental factors and lifestyle all contribute to producing chronic illness. Many diseases, including allergies, cardiovascular disease, diabetes, hypertension, mig-raines, fibromyalgia and osteoarthritis develop because a chronic inflammatory process occurs in the body.

"The increasing pain and fatigue most of us experience as we grow older is due to chronic systemic inflammation," the authors write.

Certain lifestyle factors such as prolonged stress, smoking, insufficient rest and relaxation, not enough water, and too much caffeine and alcohol can make it harder for the body to shut down inflammation. Chronic inflammation is the major factor that leads to diseased aging, according to Mr. Wassef.

His interest in complementary methods of treatment grew from of his years working alongside his dad, Lou Wassef, who has been practising pharmacy for 50 years, 33 of them in Stouffville.

After a few years of learning about medicines and helping to fill prescriptions, the younger Wassef was eventually led to the question, "Why, despite the best and most carefully selected drug therapy, do people continue to do poorly?"

FARID WASSEF

As a teenager, he endured a painful bout of osteoarthritis in his knee, brought on by sports injuries, which eventually involved operations and chronic use of anti-inflammatory medicines. That's when he was prompted to research alternate ways of healing and, by integrating other therapies, was able to heal himself to a great extent.

In the 10 years he's run his consulting practice at the pharmacy, he has witnessed some dramatic healing stories. "This is where my motivation and my excitement comes from," he said.

Whereas diseases were formerly thought to be, in large part, genetically determined, research shows people can greatly influence their health.

Mr. Wassef relates the case of a patient who went from being covered with psoriasis to having clear skin without having to take any more cortisone-based creams after a year and a half of treatment. Another person's severe autoimmune disease, which caused a painful breakdown of the connective tissues, was reversed after treatment by Mr. Wassef.

"Because it took time to develop an unhealthy state, it is going to take you some time to get well," Mr. Wassef noted.

Numerous medical practitioners have referred their patients to Mr. Wassef.

"Right now, we are not doing all we can in medicine to help improve people's health," he said.

The biggest challenge facing health care professionals in the 21st century is integrating the overwhelming amount of information that exists. "Science and medicine have become so fragmented," he said, "that we have to put it together like a jigsaw puzzle, and that is what we (the authors) have done."

Published by Viking Canada of Penguin Books, "Breaking the Age Barrier" retails at $27 and is available at all major book stores and at Houston Pharmacy in Stouffville.

> "Right now, we are not doing all we can in medicine to help improve

Step 1: Write a Press Release with a Strong Headline

You have to gain their interest so you want to capture them quickly. It should be something like this...

Local Chiropractor to Publish Book Teaching People How to Improve Their Sex Life!

There will much more on how to write a press release later in this chapter.

After the headline, you need to follow this format:

- Bold reader-focused headline.

- Mention three PAIN POINTS your readers have now.

- Talk about three GAIN POINTS your book will deliver.

- Write a clear call-to-action and offer a FREE downloadable book. *(Don't call it an eBook – downloadable version sounds so much better!)*

You need to have a single-page website called a squeeze page, opt-in page or landing page. Here's an example: www.lifemakeover31.com.

SAMPLE

FOR IMMEDIATE RELEASE

January 1, 2017
Jane Doe
Email: sample@email.com
Telephone: +1 555 1212

Local Chiropractor to Publish Book Teaching People How to Improve Their Sex Life!

People today are stressed like never before. Often within the first decade of marriage after the kids start coming, peoples' sex lives wane. They suffer from what new author Dr. Jane Bowen calls "The Droopy Drawers Syndrome." People spend money looking for answer on how to rekindle things in the bedroom, often without any real relief.

Dr. Bowen, a local chiropractor since 1998, is announcing the release of her self-published book in January 2017. "This book is a practical guidebook, a roadmap in fact," says the first-time author, "for people who have become somewhat bored in the bedroom."

Readers will learn:

- How to put some spice back into the relationship.
- 6 ways to turn on your partner.
- 5 simple techniques that will help you have a sex like you were 25 years old again.

The book will be released in six months from today and Dr. Bowen is offering readers a FREE copy of the book for a limited time. If you want to get on that list, simply go to www.drbowen.com and reserve your copy today.

PRESS RELEASE TEMPLATE

For Immediate Release
Contact: [INSERT NAME/COMPANY/TELEPHONE/EMAIL]

New book reveals _____
(INSERT THE MAIN BENEFIT OF READING YOUR BOOK, YOUR ULTIMATE PROMISE.)

Local _____ (INSERT OCCUPATION) to publish a new book entitled _____
_____ (INSERT TITLE AND TYPE IT IN ITALICS).

It will show _____ (INSERT YOUR T.POP.) how to overcome:
(INSERT 3 PAIN POINTS)

* _____

* _____

* _____

This book, to be published on _____ (INSERT DATE BOOK WILL BE PUBLISHED), will reveal practical strategies designed to help readers (INSERT 3 GAIN POINTS OR 3 THINGS THEY WILL LEARN IN THE BOOK).

* _____

* _____

* _____

In an unprecedented move, the author is offering a limited amount FREE copies of the book when it is released. To get on the waiting list, interested people should go to _____.

(INSERT A SHORT LINK TO YOUR SQUEEZE PAGE.)

_____

(INSERT A SHORT BIO - SEE SAMPLE BELOW.)

Cathy Jones is the author of the book, *Globetrotting 55+* (www.roadtripdream.com) – the ultimate road trip planning guide for extended road trips for people over 55. Cathy and her husband Larry have traveled over 150,000 road miles in the past several years, visiting all 50 states and having visited all of the national parks in the "lower 48." As national spokespeople for the RV industry, they now spend their days speaking, writing, and helping others to live their dreams.

You might find it hard to believe that this is newsworthy, but it is. Now, it's not going to be picked up by CNN for sure, but there are plenty of smaller publications that are looking for this type of thing.

Step 2: Send It Out Everywhere

Where do you send that press release to?

- Community newspapers. These are FREE local publications that often come with a slew of coupons. Make sure you focus on the fact that you are 'local'. They love giving coverage to people in their community.

- Associations. If you are a member of any professional association, they will give you publicity if you mention that you are a *member in good standing since 1999*.

- Alumni. You would be surprised that the university you graduated from is looking to brag about their students.

- Trade journals. You could get FREE press by sending this press release to journals to which you subscribe. Many of these publications have no reporters on staff so they rely on people to give them content. You will remember that many of these magazines or newspapers have a section called *People on the Move*. If they announce that so and so was promoted from supervisor to manager, trust me, they will announce that you are writing a book.

Step 3: Recycle

Recycle means reuse everywhere. Add it to your websites, blogs, social media pages. Send it to your database via post, yes, paper works like magic. They will be very impressed. Be sure to add it to your media kit too.

What do you do with this coverage?

Keep in mind that the big deal is never the appearance in the newspaper or publication. That's very short-lived. The real big benefit of being featured is that you can use that fact (and pdf copy) for years to come. Add it to your media kit. Post it on your website under a tab called *Media*. You can email it to prospects as they enter your database. You can send it to all your prospects in the mail to show them how great you are. And YOU ARE GREAT!

MAJOR CAMPAIGN:
The Interview Campaign

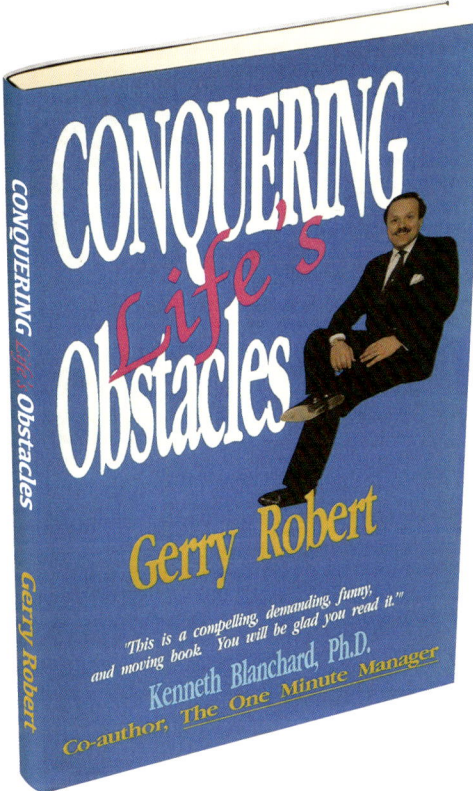

Campaign Objective: FREE publicity.

When I wrote my first book, Conquering Life's Obstacles, I was shocked by how many people wanted to interview little ol' me! I was a noboby. No one knew who I was. I was in my mid-20s. I had never achieved anything of note. I was broke. Still, I was interviewed EVERYWHERE. I couldn't understand it at first. (You don't have to understand something to benefit from it.) I later came to realize that it wasn't about me – it was about the book.

For some strange reason, in our society, the fact you're writing a book is a big deal.

How to Get Publicity and How to Use It to Catapult Your Income and Business

From Media Modest to Media Mogul: The Plan of Attack for Getting Your Name Into the Press, Without Fail.

3 Easy Steps:

1. Circle the target/study the media to become an expert.

2. Lure the prey/write a press release and contact a reporter.

3. Go in for the kill!/Give an excellent interview.

"More than 80% of the books published each year fail to break-even financially."

— Rob Eagar, author of *Sell Your Book Like Wildfire: The Writer's Guide to Marketing and Publicity*

Step 1: Circle the Target/Study the Media to Become an Expert

Before contacting the media, you have to be confident in your ability to speak as an expert. Therefore, begin by doing your research.

Be the Expert

You're in the process of, or you've already written, a book on your topic, which makes you an expert. But what's happening in the world outside of your book? You've written a book about being a successful business leader, it's great, it's polished, it's finished.

But what does being a successful business leader mean today in the world? That's something you'd better be prepared to answer, and the best way is to keep track of the news.

If you have been, then words like recession, globalization, inflation, worker productivity, the green revolution – all these might have specific meanings to you and your book.

So, you might be asking, when do I find the time to glance over the headlines of different papers, or watch dozens of national news programs, and read the most recent published journals?

One way to save a bit of time is to use the Google News service and Google News alerts. Google News is a wonderful function of the Google search engine that

> "Tell the world you're writing a book – not that you're thinking of writing a book."
>
> — Guy Kawasaki and Shawn Welch, authors of *APE: Author, Publisher, Entrepreneur - How to Publish a Book*

filters through news all over the world and brings the latest headlines, updated every few minutes. The site is usually organized by country and offers local national news, as well as global news. The site is also divided into sections, so you can click on the 'Business' tab to get the latest business news.

Google Alerts is a function found on the Google News website. If you click on the 'Google Alerts' tab, it'll bring you to a separate page. On that page, you can specify a keyword, your email address and how many times you would like to be updated. You can specify as many Google alerts as you want, so you can have a whole variety of words like: 'Leadership', 'Merger', 'Employment', 'Productivity' or whatever words capture your interest.

Elevator Speech

After you've done your research, you have to feel confident speaking about your topic. Having a prepared speech can give you that extra edge when speaking with journalists or anyone else interested in your book.

Now that you've done your research, you should be prepared to talk to anyone and anybody about your book. Networking is a powerful tool, and you never know when opportunities might surface. Maybe you'll run into the local business reporter while at the bank. You might meet the president of your local rotary club at a soccer game.

In the classic example, a CEO of a well-known company is in the elevator next to you. There are a lot of directors, associate directors and managers who work for that CEO. In fact, all those people could benefit from your book and perhaps your seminar.

So WHAT are you going to say?

Have a short rehearsed line that will get people's attention. A classic way journalists focus their stories is by writing just a sentence, using this skeleton: People doing something for a reason. You can apply this same thought pattern to your book by asking these questions:

- Who is the book addressing?

- What do these people need to learn?

- Why do they need to learn it?

You might want to introduce your book by establishing it as a solution to a common problem in business today. Probably you've gotten this information because you've been following the news, and you've tapped into somebody else's research findings.

Statistics can be a great way to open the doors to conversation, or to use when approaching the media!

Step 2: Lure the Prey/Write a Press Release and Media Kit

You know you've got information to offer to the media. But how do you get the media interested in what you've got to say? First off, write a press release.

5 Strategies for Writing a Book Announcement Press Release That Will Get You FREE Publicity!

A book announcement press release helps us tell the world our new book is available for purchase. It's often sent to the media with a copy of the book or a note asking if the journalist would like to receive a complimentary review copy. It's also included in the book's media kit.

In today's world, if you don't write the press release the right way, it'll just be filed in the circular file box known as the *garbage* or *trash* can on the computer. It's important to understand how to write a release that will get read and used.

Here are key strategies designed to help you avoid common mistakes:

1. **Use the traditional news release format.** This includes your contact information, a headline and your announcement written in a journalistic style. Study the press releases at www.prweb.com and www.prnewswire.com for examples. Don't use graphics, multiple columns, or different fonts sizes and colours.

2. **It's about the book, not you.** Remember that you are not the news. Your book is the big deal. Unless your name is Trump, Branson, Gates, don't put it in the headline. "New book reveals how teenagers can avoid being bullied" is more compelling than, "Mary Jones' new book is about bullying." No one cares about you (except me and your mom) or your book… they care about themselves and their challenges.

3. **Avoid using superlatives.** A news release announces news in a factual way, so limit your descriptive text to the facts. This isn't a book review expressing an opinion – it's an announcement that a journalist would like to copy and paste into a publication. That's why you want to avoid language – 'fabulous', 'best-ever', 'fascinating' – that you won't see in a news story.

4. **Distribute your announcement release in text format, not as a PDF file.** It is easy to copy and paste text from an email or from a website; it is hard to copy text from a PDF file. The more you make somebody work to use your information, the less likely they are to do so.

5. **Tell us where to buy the book or better still, tell us where we can get a FREE copy**. Because we know the big money in book publishing is not from book but from the business around the book, giving it away for FREE has amazing power to fill your database with hot prospects.

The Main Parts of a Killer Press Release Headline

The headline is the ad for the piece. You need to attract the editors to read more. Controversy and/or questions work best. Be creative and have fun with it! When you've decided on a descriptive, clever and catchy headline, type it in bold and strong fonts, and center it. Your sub-headline, which should be placed directly below the headline, is a summary line that explains quickly the main point of the press release. It is best to write the body of the press release before writing the headline and sub-headline.

Needs and Problems

The lead paragraph is designed to invite the reader into the article. It should have a broad appeal. Your first line should identify a large problem of your target population, and you should demonstrate that you have a solution to this problem. Make a case for why it is important to solve this problem.

Even better, see if you're addressing a problem that is currently being discussed by the media; make your solution a unique answer that offers fresh perspective.

For instance:

Most marriages break up because of money problems, but author Doug Welpton says approaching money problems in the right way can make a relationship stronger.

Development

Add a second paragraph to develop the message. Elaborate on the problem. Is there a statistic to back up your statement? Did Harvard release a study on marital problems that says 80% of marriages break up because of finances? Put the most interesting information first to keep the reader interested.

Readers and reporters have short attention spans; keep them interested! Recite the most important items in descending order so that if some are cut from the end, the most important will remain. Keep in mind that the media love statistics or survey results of any kind.

The Book as a Problem-Solver

Now move from a problem to a solution orientation. Provide your personal solution, pulling pointers from your book. Generally, three suggestions is a good number. Give three detailed and descriptive points that anyone can apply to everyday life which support your solution. Make sure to mention that these pointers are found in your book, and that your book is a resource to assist people's problem solving.

Author Biography

Aside from being an author, give your other expertise here; what have you done in the past? Tell them who you are and why you are qualified to address this issue.

Media Information

How can a reporter contact you? It is always best to give a phone number, followed by an email, followed by a website address.

You've got a killer press release. Next, study media venues to find out where you should be sending your press release.

FOR IMMEDIATE RELEASE

January 1, 2017
Jane Doe
Email: sample@email.com
Telephone: +1 555 1212

Protect your home... consult a thief

Local author interviews retired robbers on how to protect homes. Last year in Oshawa, more than 3,000 families returned home to find their personal belongings strewn throughout their house. In fact, police say home robberies in the city increased 30 percent in 2015 over 2014.

It's the reason Jane Doe has written the book, *How I Can Break into Your House: A Robber's Guide to Security*. After being a victim of a home robbery herself, despite having what she believed was the latest in high-tech security, she slept for weeks with one eye open.

It was important for her to find out how thieves were circumventing home alarm systems. In her book, she has interviewed 20 professional thieves, who have since retired from their criminal careers.

They have told Doe:

- A dark home is their delight, no matter what security system the home has.
- Their worst fear is a barking dog.
- The most common place they found jewellery was in a top drawer.

This book has already helped many people rethink what they do before they leave their home for the day. *How I Can Break into Your House: A Robber's Guide to Security* is available at www.howicanbreakinto.com. Doe is available for an interview to discuss other ways local residents can protect themselves against this increasing trend of home robberies.

Media Information
   Jane Doe, sample@email.com, +1 555 1212

Research Your Niche

Before you send out your press release, know which forms of media you are approaching. There are a variety of newspapers, magazines, radio and television programs out there, many of them niche.

Find out which magazines specialize in self-help. Perhaps there is a local television program that specializes in finances. Many newspapers have separate business, health and entertainment sections. Make a list of these specific media venues you would like to approach. Then, research these venues. Most media outlets have websites; skim the website for articles and content.

Find a Contact

The easiest way to find contact information for newspapers, radio stations, etc. is to search the website. For newspapers, often the managing editors and the section editors can be found under a specific "Contact Us" heading. Most journalists have what is called a beat; this means that the journalist has become an expert in one area and writes articles relating to this area. For example, each newspaper will have a health reporter or municipal reporter, who writes articles specially on health or city council.

Often, you can find the emails for beat reporters on the website. Some media websites may even specify a special process for submitting news releases. Secure a name and email address.

Email Your Press Release

Many editors and reporters are very busy and won't take the time to open an attachment, so include your release in the body of your email along with your introduction letter. The more direct your approach, the better. Remember, newspapers will be interested in printing an article if you approach them as an author who provides a solution to a current issue/problem discussed in the media.

Example Email Messages

Dear Alva,
As a long-time resident of Markham, I am a dedicated reader of The Markham Sun and am always interested in the news of my community. I am also the author of Beating the Bank and a financial expert who gives advice on how individuals can turn debt around.

Currently, 80% of Markham residents are living beyond their means. I have provided a press release below, which discusses what local residents need to do to get out of debt.

Thank you,
[insert your name and contact here]

Dear Henry Carter,
As the published author of Beating the Bank and a financial expert, I am concerned with the current struggle of individuals who find themselves in debt. Please find below a press release, which gives simple advice to help individuals increase their finances. I would be happy to provide my expertise or be available for an interview upon request.

Thank you,
[insert your name and contact here]

Radio and Television

For radio and television, you will do better to contact first by phone and then by follow-up email. By leaving a phone message, the producer or scout for the show will be able to evaluate your voice and your media presence. Sound confident, enthusiastic and like the expert you are! In terms of content and what you say, offer your book as a packaged show. If you appear on the television program, can you do a 'financial makeover' of an individual? Follow up your phone call with an email, offering your press release.

> "All publicity is good, except an obituary notice."
>
> — Brendan Behan, playwright

Follow-Up

Call a few days later to make sure the press release was received.

Where to begin? *New York Times* or *Dog River Times*? When you begin publicizing yourself, it's always best to begin local and build your portfolio.

Starting Local

The best place to begin is with your own local media. Prepare a general news release for your local newspaper, magazine or radio personality. It is BIG NEWS in a community when a local resident and author publishes something.

So if you've written a book on business, contact the local business reporter. Let him or her know that you admire the articles he or she writes. Mention that you're an expert, that you've written a book, and that you'd be happy to meet.

Journalists are always looking for an expert to quote and for story ideas.

As someone who has just written a book, you can offer both. Tell the reporter that you'd be happy to be a source anytime he or she needs an expert to talk to about business ventures. If he or she wanted to write an article on your book too, you'd be happy to supply the press release to him or her and to answer any questions. Talk about your book with the reporter.

Use those great statistics you have to introduce the book; use your elevator speech. Get him or her interested in your work because you HAVE done something interesting!

The Offer of Expertise

Target your media more effectively by identifying your market (this is not to say, however, that your book cannot be topical for a wide variety of markets). For example, find a business magazine and pitch yourself to them as a guest columnist. If there is a radio program on finances, contact the host of that show and offer your expertise on their program.

Remember, you are an 'expert' in your field, even if your book has not been printed yet.

Even better, suggest story or column ideas when you approach these venues. If you tell the editor of the magazine you'd love to write a column on 'managing the monthly bills', on 'the seven common qualities of a leader' or on 'making a $20 bill stretch'... that editor will probably be more interested. It's helpful to offer a brief summary as well.

To further the offer of expertise, use Google Alerts, or follow the news to see what's been written and by who, and then you can offer your advice as a follow-up.

> "Expertise builds credibility. Credibility builds trust. Trust breeds comfort and confidence. Comfort and confidence breed book sales. Any questions?"
>
> — Rob Eagar, author of *Sell Your Book Like Wildfire: The Writer's Guide to Marketing and Publicity*

For example, if you've written a book on increasing worker happiness and you see an article on poor workplace morale, contact the journalist who wrote the article and pitch your advice and your book as a follow-up solution. People who are happier at home and with their lives, in general, make better employees.

Find statistics to back up your statement: It is shown that people who are happier with their lives are 90% more productive in their place of employment. See where your 'story' fits into the national dialogue around you or how you can insert it into that dialogue. Find an angle that you can work to your advantage.

Go Big and Then Go Home

Now that you've built a portfolio, you're ready to break into the national media. To do this, use your other media experience to establish your credibility. If you've appeared in the *Dog River Times*, and on 92.9 Talk Radio's *Finances with Freddy*, and have appeared on Cable 10's show, *Your Money*, and wrote a column for *Monthly Money Matters*, when it comes time to contact the journalist of the *New York Times*, say that you've been written up in newspapers, have appeared on radio and television programs, and have written a column for a business journal. Tell that journalist that you admire his or her work, and forward your press release to him or her.

This time, though, you'll be using your news research to your advantage. Journalists write articles if the topic is timely, significant and interesting. So show how your book is timely, significant and interesting. For instance, it's timely that the economy is geared potentially for a recession. So show how your book is significant as a safeguard for companies and their management teams. Show how your book is interesting and how it taps into solving a national problem in a new, unique, innovative way.

You've written a book to be proud of, and something that deserves the attention of the world. So go get it!

GERRY ROBERT | 167

OUR CLIENT CASE STUDY

Author   : Alexander Woo
Title   : *Work Hard, Die Poor? Or Work Smart, Retire Young & Rich*
Occupation : Entrepreneur
Location   : Kuala Lumpur, Malaysia
Website   : www.facebook.com/worksmartbook
Win   : Alexander uses his book to gain massive publicity for his business. He never received any publicity prior to publishing his book with Black Card Books. He is a serial entrepreneur and has a number of companies.

"The media constantly needs stories for its publications and shows. According to radio expert Alex Carroll, 'Radio needs 10,000 guests every day to fill up the airways.' So, the media needs you."

— Rick Frishman and Robyn Freedman Spizman, authors of *Author 101 Bestselling Book Publicity*

Step 3: Go In for the Kill!/Give an Excellent Interview

You've sent in your press release, and now you're waiting to hear back from the reporters. There's a lot you can do before, during and after the interview, which will ensure your name looks great in print.

Preparing for the Media Interview

Items to Consider for Media Preparation

This is a list of items and ideas to help you prepare and be ready for any publicity opportunity that may arise now or in the future. It will also help you draft press releases as the news happens and/or news items that may pop up from time to time as they relate to your book topic:

1. Release date of the book.

2. Provide a brief bio/résumé or, if available, both.

3. List any trade publications to which you subscribe.

4. List any relevant associations that you belong to.

5. Do you have experience doing media interviews?

6. List your volunteer experience.

7. What is exceptional about you? What makes you different or unique? (Remember, they are looking for a hook to generate media interest.)

Dean got 1,200 leads in a single 90-minute radio interview. Don't try telling him that it's not worth pursuing media attention. This works the same way for those who have never been interviewed.

8. Do you have any of your own ideas on how you would like your publicity to be handled?

9. Would you be interested in doing book signings?

10. Do you have any event ideas that could coincide with your book release?

11. What is your local bookstore?

12. Name some of the media sources you specifically read or listen to.

13. Give a couple of key quotes from your book that you see as controversial or unique to your subject.

14. Please list keywords for media searches that pertain to your book.

Know What the Reporter Expects

Remember, the reporter is not there to be your friend or to help promote your business. They are there for a story and some good quotes and background for the story. Don't expect them to help you. Meanwhile, your media kit, which you should have done by now, will help you supply the reporter with great background material on you and your business.

Be Interesting or Be Invisible

Reporters will use such background material to help give you credibility and identify you to the reader. Reporters like to visit you at your home or place of business. Remember, reporters are trained to observe everything they see and write it down either now or later when they write the story.

Be aware of your surroundings and consider if they are orderly and neat. Dress appropriately for the interview. Consider it to be similar to a job interview. First impressions are critical and they seem to last forever. Give them something positive to write about. (Reporters often prefer a quiet, private space to do the interview so there are no interruptions. If it's your place, then try to look at it objectively or ask a friend or colleague to help you out. They may be able to see things you didn't even notice.) They may also want to take a picture rather than use your own business-approved photo. Some reporters will, however, use it if it is a particularly good one.

Know Your Stuff!

Learn your key messages. Develop questions and answers. (Some websites have a tab called FAQs – frequently asked questions. They have anticipated some possible questions the public might need answered beforehand.) You can even give the reporter a copy of some questions and answers if you can anticipate some questions they will ask you.

Make sure you know who will be asking the questions and even ask the reporter who else will be interviewed for the story. Be familiar with the publication and try to find out something about their readership, even circulation numbers. If it's only you then all the better, as this will be your moment to shine.

Consider:

Who is your audience? Remember to talk through the reporter to your public. They are your target.

What do they need to know?

What are they likely to misunderstand? (If you are aware of any glitches, do not be afraid to confront them and offer your explanation to the reporter. It's better to confront them. Address them. Solve them and offer solutions. This is far better than being caught off-guard later on.)

Prepare for any possible tough questions. Ask a friend or colleague to brainstorm with you about possible questions, and write them down and answer them. Later, in your next interview, you may be more prepared as a result of this exercise.

Commonly Asked Questions:

1. Why did you decide to write the book?

2. What makes you an expert?

3. Who is the book written for?

4. What is the main message of your book?

5. Does it offer a solution?

6. How will local audiences (radio station audiences, newspaper readers) relate to your book?

7. What can they learn?

8. If your book offers a solution, can you give specific examples of people who have used your advice to better their lives?

9. Have you used your own advice?

10. Do you have statistics to back up your book?

11. What are the contrasting views?

During the Interview

You're so close now you just have to talk to the reporter! Above all, remember to remain relaxed. After all, you are the expert, and you know more about your topic than the reporter.

Golden Rules for the Interview

1. There is no such thing as "off the record."

2. "No comment" is never the right answer.

3. Omit jargon and acronyms; speak plainly so that an eight-year-old can understand you.

4. Focus on the human-interest angle. You'll be most appealing to your target market if you convey real, human empathy. So be passionate about your message because you want to help people!

What to Expect/Be Prepared for

1. If you don't know the answer to something, don't try to fake it. Just say you don't know, that it's not your area of expertise but you will volunteer to get the answer for them. Also, never assume the reporter understands everything you say. Don't get too technical and, again, keep it simple and straightforward.

2. Watch your body language and facial expressions as they tell a reporter volumes about you without you even being aware of them.

3. Again, assume everything you say is 'on the record' even when the reporter puts away the tape recorder or the notepad and pen. Always assume they are still reporting even if the conversation at the end turns light and personal.

4. If you do a phone interview and the reporter catches you off-guard, tell them you are in the middle of something but that you will call them back at a specified time, depending on their deadline. Just explain that you want to make sure you have all the correct information you will need on hand. If possible, it would be a good idea

to try and return media calls within two hours. Believe me, they will move on to the next interviewee on their list as they are often pressed to meet deadlines.

5. Don't forget to get the reporter's name, contact information and their deadline.

6. If you can, ask the reporter what information he or she is seeking and what information they have already obtained, and how your information will be used. Ask if they want a simple quote for a short news story or an extensive background for a feature article.

7. Take time to prepare. Review your key messages and your prepared questions and answers. Be aware of the reporter's deadline, but only do the interview when you are ready.

8. Use point-form notes, but only as a reference. You don't want to appear to be reading your answers or searching for a response. Relax! Breathe slowly and deeply. Sip some water before the interview. It keeps your throat from drying (coffee has the opposite effect, I've found). Take your time. Don't rush your response. REMEMBER, YOU KNOW MORE ABOUT THE SUBJECT THAN THE REPORTER EVER WILL.

9. 'People stories' always make for the most interesting interviews. Give examples of real person scenarios to back up your points. This will connect you with the audience and with the reporter.

10. While you should think about the human-interest value of your story, do have some statistics to back up your argument. Word statistics in a way that people can easily grasp your idea (for example: In a percentage, say double or half instead of 'Out of 333, 155 people believe...').

Key: Don't Push Your Book. Push an Interesting Topic.

11. When you think you've answered a question adequately, don't feel compelled to keep talking just because there is a microphone up to your mouth. If you're satisfied with your answer, sit in silence. Rambling leads you to say the wrong thing. Think before you speak. Avoid fillers such as 'uh', 'ah', 'well', 'yeah' and 'you know'.

Remember, it is the reporter's job to keep the interview going. He or she will fill in the silences; it is not your responsibility.

Never answer with just 'yes' or 'no.' If you are asked a yes or no question, try to answer with 'Yes, because…' or 'No, because…'

"You cannot spend one hour a week on promotional activities and expect to grow."

— Rob Eagar, author of *Sell Your Book Like Wildfire: The Writer's Guide to Marketing and Publicity*

Tips for Radio Interviews:

1. You may have to go into a studio, or you may have to do the interview over the phone.

2. Be aware that radio reporters may or MAY NOT ask to tape an interview over the telephone. The reporter should tell you before the taping begins, but you should ALWAYS ASSUME that taping begins when the conversation begins.

3. Breathe deeply from the diaphragm, so that your voice projects more.

4. Talk with a smile on your face, and talk very enthusiastically. You may feel silly, but the more enthusiastic you are, the more interesting your voice will be to listen to.

> *"You can overcome a person's skepticism by showing how you can improve his life. It's hard for people to feel antagonistic when they realize you're trying to help them."*
>
> — Rob Eagar, author of *Sell Your Book Like Wildfire: The Writer's Guide to Marketing and Publicity*

Be prepared. If you have written something controversial in your book, be prepared to defend it as it will most likely be asked about.

If you are doing television or radio interviews, be sure to occassionally refer back to your book when giving an answer. Example question: What was the most difficult time in your life? Answer: Well, as I wrote in my book, it was when my father told me I would never be successful.

Don't give long, detailed answers. The more variety of information you can give, the better the story or interview. Remember, the reporter only has limited space in print, or airtime… make your answers brief and allow them to get as many questions in as possible.

Don't refuse to answer a question unless it is totally unrelated to you or your book. For example, if you are writing about healthcare and the reporter asks what political party you support, turn the question into your favour. Your answer could be: "Regardless of who I support, and I think they both have valid healthcare plans, the voting public is in danger of a crisis."

Do learn how to conduct yourself well by watching as many television interviews as you can. Ask yourself how you would answer some of the more generic questions.

Do practice in front of a mirror and in front of a friend.

Final tip: Be sure to ask when the article will appear/when the segment will be aired. Then watch it, read it and see for yourself how you can work the magic. Then, prepare yourself to do it all over again.

Rapid Fire Tips

Always know your Primary Objective (P.O.) of the interview. What are you looking to get out of this interview? If you are there to fill a seminar you are presenting, then lock into that in your mind. If the reporter takes you off-track, you can always bring them back on topic… your FREE seminar tonight at the Marriott Hotel. Send a Personal Handwritten Note (PHN) to the producer and reporter immediately after the interview. It will make you stand out like crazy and they will remember you next time you need publicity.

Always offer an Attraction Marketing Device (AMD). Be sure to offer a FREE book, a FREE home study course, a second opinion, FREE ticket on each interview. Direct them to your landing page where they can access the FREE offer. Don't ask for permission to do this, just do it.

The Power of an Upcoming Book

Several years ago, when the hit movie *THE SECRET* was in its heyday, I was business partners with the star of the movie, Bob Proctor. We were in Florida doing a seminar and we got a call from the *Larry King Live* show. They wanted Bob to appear the following day in California. So we chartered a private jet to fly us from Florida to Toronto, then from there to Los Angeles, then to Calgary then back home to Toronto.

Before I left Los Angeles, I wanted to get publicity for Bob before we arrived in Calgary. So I sent the Calgary media a press release with the headline Bob Proctor, star of the hit movie *THE SECRET*, fresh from an appearance on the *Larry King Live* show last night, coming to Calgary, available for media interviews. *No One Called.*

That really annoyed me so I resent the press release with one small change:

Bob Proctor, star of the hit movie *THE SECRET*, fresh from an appearance on the *Larry King Live* show last night, to publish a new book entitled *CREATE YOUR OWN ECONOMY*, coming to Calgary, available for media interviews. THE PHONE RANG OFF THE WALL… Only difference? I mentioned his upcoming book.

OUR CLIENT CASE STUDY

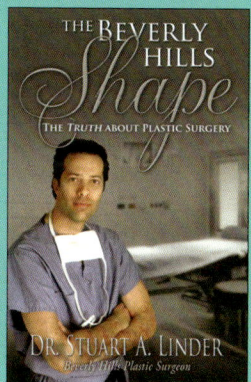

Author : Stuart Linder, MD
Title : *The Beverly Hills Shape: The Truth About Plastic Surgery*
Occupation : Plastic Surgeon
Location : Beverly Hills, California
Website : www.drlinder.com
Win : Here is one of the best examples that I've ever seen in using a book to get publicity. I published this book in 2007. Dr. Linder has appeared on *20/20* with Barbara Walters, *TMZ, Dr. Oz, Entertainment Tonight, The View, Fox News, The Hollywood Reporter*, and in *Star Magazine, Cosmopolitan, Allure, Glamour* and on and on and on.

Use a professionally designed media kit to show the media you are a PLAYER!

Prepare it in PDF 8.5" x 11" or A4 Size.

Follow this template exactly.

POWERED BY black card BOOKS — media kit

CHRISTINE LOUIS DE CANONVILLE

The THREE FACES Of EVIL

UNMASKING THE FULL SPECTRUM OF NARCISSISTIC ABUSE

media kit
CHRISTINE LOUIS DE CANONVILLE

THE BOOK

DESCRIPTION

The 21st Century has brought with it a narcissistic epidemic, and a flood of traumatised victims that end up in the therapy room. Unfortunately, Narcissistic Abuse and Narcissistic Victim Syndrom (NVS) are subjects that most therapists are unaware of, leaving them ill-equipped for recognizing and working with victims suffering from this devastating form of abuse that strips them of their identity.

From the boardroom to the bedroom, narcissists are everywhere. They can be parents, partners, friends, bosses, siblings; no one is safe. This form of abuse goes way beyond physical and psychological injury — it strikes at the very soul of the victim, leaving them wondering whether they are literally going mad.

It is imperative for everyone to understand the relationship dynamics that exists between the narcissist and their victims, i.e. their need for entitlement, control, power, grandiosity, and specialness. Also, to understand how a narcissist uses seduction and manipulation to "hook" their victims into a dangerous liaison.

The Three Faces of Evil is not only a primer for therapists, but is written for everybody, especially those survivors wanting to understand what happened to them while in a relationship with a perpetrator.

This book will educate and familiarize the reader about the complexity of narcissistic behaviours, giving a basic understanding of The Dark Triad: from Narcissistic Personality Disorder, Malignant Narcissism, to the most pathological: The Psychopath.

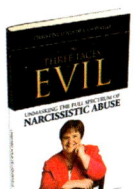

Learn How To...

- Spot these predators before they spot you, because that is the only way to stay safe.

Make sure that this document is branded in a way that matches your book cover.

Have a professional take your pictures and insert high-resolution pictures of yourself.

THE BOOK

media kit
CHRISTINE LOUIS DE CANONVILLE

Show people how your book will help readers.

UNCOVER IN THESE PAGES...

- Ways to spot a predator before they spot you.
- How to identify a narcissist's mind games.
- The characteristics of a manipulative personality.
- The extreme behaviour of the Jekyll & Hyde personality.
- Twenty strategies for recognizing the "red flags" that signal danger.
- The characteristics of the Dark Triad Personalities: (Narcissism, Machiavellianism, and Psychopathy)
- How narcissists use seduction and manipulation to groom their victims.
- The psychological and emotional abuse of Gaslighting on the victim.
- Insights into the symptoms of Narcissistic Victim Syndrome.
- How to STOP being a victim, and becoming a narcissistic supply.

Anyone can learn how to spot a predator if they have the right tools.

Find a quote from your book.

"Gaslighting is a form of psychological abuse used by narcissists in order to instill in their victims an extreme sense of anxiety and confusion to the point where they no longer trust their own judgment."

—CHRISTINE LOUIS DE CANONVILLE

Follow this template exactly. Use the same amount of bullet points.

THE AUTHOR

Christine Louis de Canonville, B.A. Hons; MIACP; MTCI; MPNLP, CMH; CHyp has been a psychotherapist and supervisor of mental health professionals for over 20 years. She worked in the trauma unit of a psychiatric hospital, and worked specifically with victims of narcissistic abuse in her private practice for many years.

Christine has recognized a gap in the training of many psychotherapists—this book sets out to address the shortfalls in a therapist's education so that they become better equipped to work with survivors of narcissistic abuse. As part of her health advocacy work she set up her website www.narcissisticbehavior.net where she posts original and much needed information for educating both therapists and survivors. She went on to develop an effective programme for working one-to-one with victims suffering from Narcissistic Victim Syndrome, and developed workshops for educating therapists and other health professionals in the whole spectrum of narcissistic abuse.

Much of her knowledge has come from her postgrad studies in Criminology and Forensic Psychology, and it is through these disciplines that she has gained her understanding of the The Dark Triad, (Narcissism, Machiavellianism, and Psychopathy). These Three Faces of Evil are vital information for understanding the full spectrum of narcissistic abuse.

It is her vision that narcissistic abuse becomes part of the curriculum of all Mental Health Professionals as well as those in related disciplines (i.e. Psychotherapists, Social Workers, Police, Doctors, Solicitors, Law Courts, HR management, etc.) who deal with the fallout of this form of abuse.

Write a strong author bio.

180 | MOVE IT

Testimonials are VERY Powerful. Use them if you have them.

TESTIMONIALS

"This is an engaging introduction to the increasingly popular subject of narcissistic abuse. It is comprehensive, detailed, and written with both therapists and victims in mind. I believe that it is a book that everybody should read."

Cynthia Davis, author of *In Search of Wisdom*

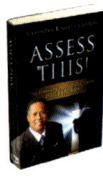

"Christine Louis de Canonville has provided a tremendously important tool for understanding the full scope of narcissism for both victims and professionals. I recommend it highly."

Alexander Figueroa, author of *Assess This!*

"A small book packed with fascinating and useful information regarding all aspects of narcissistic behaviour that therapists will find themselves going back to time and time again. A great resource for therapists and victims alike."

Patsy Chia, Author of *Burden No More*

Media Kit 5

TESTIMONIALS

"All professionals involved in working with victims of abuse will find much value in the pages of this book, and it really should be required reading for every psychotherapist in training."

Berns Dawn Lucases, Author of *Time Is Up!*

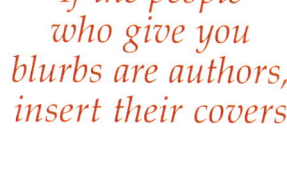

If the people who give you blurbs are authors, insert their covers.

"Narcissism is one of the most prevalent personality disorders of our time, yet Christine Louis de Canonville has drawn together a practical and accessible book that covers all aspects of the behaviour. It is written in a language that anybody can read for steering them through the narcissism maze."

Franky Ronaldy & Meow Ling Ng, Author of *Life Sucks!*

"*The Three Faces of Evil: Unmasking the Full Spectrum of Narcissistic Abuse* is true to its title. The outstanding text focuses on empirically based evidence that reveals comprehensive insight into the dark triad of narcissistic personality, malignant narcissism, and psychopathy. This volume should be part of every psychotherapist's reading matter."

Caroline Bachot, Author of *The Fastest Way to Happiness*

182 | MOVE IT

media kit
CHRISTINE LOUIS DE CANONVILLE

BOOK INFO

This data is vital.

Make sure you get an ISBN number.

Book Title:	The Three Faces of Evil
Subtitle:	Unmasking the Full Spectrum of Narcissistic Abuse
Release Date:	April 2015
Price:	USD 32.00
ISBN:	978-1-77204-146-0
Phone Number:	00 353 1 282 3685
E-mail Address:	christine@narcissisticbehavior.net
Website:	www.narcissisticbehavior.net

Publisher
Black Card Books
Suite 214
5-18 Ringwood Drive
Stouffville, Ontario
Canada, L4A 0N2
Tel: +1 877 280 8536
www.blackcardbooks.com

Insert your contact info on the last page.

OUR CLIENT CASE STUDY

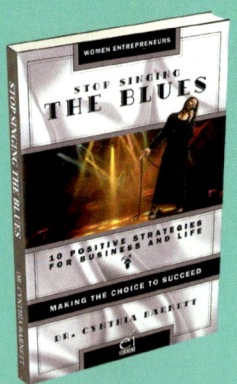

Author : Cynthia Barnett
Title : *Stop Singing The Blues*
Occupation : Speaker and Coach
Location : Norwalk, Connecticut
Website : www.refiredontretire.com
Win : Our client Cynthia Barnett struck GOLD when she appeared in *Time Magazine* in 2005. She was an educator her whole career and launched into coaching and speaking after she retired from teaching. Just imagine how her new coaching practice grew with national coverage. That's the power of a book.

"With advertising, you pay for it; with publicity, you pray for it."

— Rick Frishman and Robyn Freedman Spizman, authors of *Author 101 Bestselling Book Publicity*

Use HARO

HARO stands for HELP A REPORTER OUT. Go over to www.helpareporter.com. This site is incredible for getting interviews and it's FREE. Here's how it works:

The website has two parts. One for reporters and one for experts and authors. When a reporter is assigned an article to write, they need content. They go to this website and type in what kind of help they need and what the story is about. You, as an author, receive emails detailing exactly what the reporter is looking for what the story is about, who to contact and the deadline. This is incredible. This is precisely how I got Cynthia Barnett into *Time Magazine*.

MISC CAMPAIGNS

OUR CLIENT CASE STUDY

Author : James Burgess
Title : *CHAOS – How Business Leaders Can Master The Power of Focus*
Occupation: Management Consultant
Location : Toronto, Canada
Website : www.Focus31.com
Win : James uses his book to get non-paid speaking engagements in front of the Chamber of Commerce groups. They promote the event and get higher attendance because an author is coming to deliver a speech. Anywhere from 20 to 150 people show up. James offers a next to FREE two-day class and it's at that class that he sells his $3,000 Accountability Coaching Service. He routinely earns over $10,000 in a day.

1. Sell Books at Speaking Engagements.

There are no shortcuts in public speaking. You have to develop your skills and, yes, anyone can learn how to become a good speaker. If you are serious about becoming a professional speaker you must get trained. There are many awesome speaker trainers and I would be happy to recommend some if you need experts. Just send an email to gerry@blackcardbooks.com and ask for SPEAKER TRAINING RECOMMENDATIONS.

One of the best organizations is Toastmasters International (www.toastmasters.org). This is a worldwide not-for-profit organization designed to teach people how to speak in public and become an awesome communicator and leader. It's dirt-cheap to join. Most cities have numerous groups running each week. You can visit for FREE and trust me, you'll be warmly welcomed. I had the pleasure of being the closing keynote speaker at their international convention almost 30 years ago. I recommend them everywhere I go.

Another thing I recommend is studying what the real pros do. If someone is earning over $1,000,000 per year in the speaking business *(I generate multiple millions per month now in sales)*, nothing happens by accident. Study everything. Their movements, their close, their humour, everything. I remember watching a speaker's close in a video. His pitch was about 45 minutes long. I watched and rewatched it for five hours.

2. Speak for FREE.

There are hundreds if not thousands of opportunities for new speakers to present every month. When you are an author, there is no such thing as speaking for FREE. At the very least, if you can sell your book at the end of your talk, you will earn something. Keep in mind that in every audience, between a third to half of the crowd will buy your book. If you are speaking to 200 people and 100 buy your book at $34, that's $3,400. Not bad for an hour of talking! Do that a few times a month and you're off to the races.

Contact all of the service clubs in your area (Rotary, Chamber of Commerce, Lions, etc.). Tell them you want to speak and you are willing to forgo your fee in exchange for the opportunity to sell your book for a few minutes at the end of your talk.

Offer to speak for FREE to conventions, conferences, not-for-profits and corporate events. Always send them an invoice with a FREE – NICE GUY DISCOUNT – on the invoice that has your normal fee. It should be no less than $3,000 for a keynote speech.

3. Learn to Sell from the Stage.

You can be the best speaker in the world but if you can't sell from the stage, you'll be a great (broke) speaker, and there are plenty of them, let me tell you. Study the big guns in speaking. Watch how many times they seed their close within the body of their talk. Watch how they subtly sell themselves to the audience. Look at the body language and when they use it. This isn't a book on how to become a speaker, but I wanted to include this here because I see so many authors who just love

BECOME ONE OF MY SPEAKERS!

www.publishabookandgrowrich.com/lss

to speak and they don't sell very well. I routinely sell over $1,000,000 in a weekend. That's because I work on myself all of the time and I've studied the biggest players and deconstructed everything they do.

4. Sell, Sell, Sell and All Will Be Well, Well, Well!

I suggest holding your book and referring to it frequently in your talk. Quote from it. Tell them that this next point comes from page… When it comes to moving books at talks, my recommendation is that you give a bonus that exceeds the price of your book. This must be something that's low-cost to you but high perceived cost to them. It could be a FREE consultation, or FREE home study course, or FREE 2nd opinion, or FREE coaching session, or do what T. Harv Eker does for his blockbuster hit, *Secrets of the Millionaire Mind*: He offers two FREE tickets to his seminar.

Also, give them a price discount off the suggested retail printed on the back of the book. Say your book has a $44 price printed on the cover, offer it for $30 but if they buy two copies, it's only $38. That's $19 each. Let's say your book costs you $3 to print, that's a whopping $16 profit for you. If you sell 200 copies, that's almost $4,000 to you.

When you are on the stage, you could do what I do at the end of each of my seminars: I tell the audience that I want to close by reading a story from my book, *The Millionaire Mindset*. Before I read the story, I sell the book. I go over some of the chapters and always relate it to their pain. Then I clearly tell them my CTA (Call-to-Action) and what I want them to do when I'm done. You must give crystal-clear instructions. Tell them everything… Okay, you want to be filling out the order form now. Print clearly and when I'm done, you want to come back here with me… point to the back… say, "See that lady at the back, that's Mary… Mary, wave your hand and say hi to Mary, everyone. You will give her the order form, she will give you a book and you want to get that signed by me today. Remember, I only have 12 FREE consultations available so you need to jump on this quickly as soon as I'm done."

OUR CLIENT CASE STUDY

Author : John Salton
Title : *Get the Renovation You Really Want!*
Occupation : Home Renovator
Location : Perth, Australia
Win : John got several speaking engagements at home shows. They loved it because they got an author to speak at the show and he loved it because after the lecture, he would tell people that he was a renovator and – get this – one who wrote the book on how to get the renovation you really, really want. He told me that it brought in an additional $2,000,000 of additional business within the first year of using his book to build his business.

5. Sell Special Editions of Your Book.

I once was involved in publishing a special edition of a book. We were commissioned by Purina Pet Foods to analyze what veterinarians were doing wrong and how we could help them make more money. We discovered that they were lousy at retailing food, supplements and other services in their clinics. So we wrote a great book to help vets do a better job at retailing in their clinics.

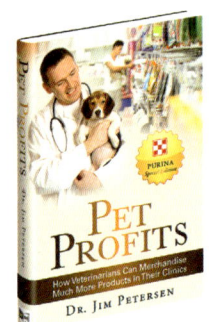

When we published the book, we printed the Purina logo on the cover and called it the Purina Special Edition. On the front page of the book, we had a letter from the CEO explaining the book and how it could help vets. Then they mailed a FREE copy to 30,000 veterinarians in North America. Yes, 30,000 copies.

One way to help you do this is to interview CEOs of large companies as you are writing your book. This is no guarantee but let me tell you, it significantly increases your chances if you interview the CEO and then say something nice about them as you share their wisdom in your book.

A few years later, we had a similar thing happen with Pampers and a book I published called *Gentle Hands* by Susan Harley of Perth, Australia. Her book teaches parents how to massage newborn babies. After some selling, she was asked for a proposal from Pampers who wanted to buy 200,000 copies of her book.

6. Plant People in Your Book.

One way to move books, or at least significantly increase the likelihood of it, is to do what our client Rev. Larry Marshall did for his book, *It's Your Wedding*. Larry's book was designed to help people plan a perfect wedding. For years, he married people. When his book was ready for release, I told him to get consent to put full-page wedding pictures of people he had married *(and were still together!)*. By having two dozen couples in his book, he was able to approach those couples and offer them a case of books at a discount. Many bought the case because their pictures were in the book.

The best way to plant people in your book is for you to interview them. Simply tell them that you are completing the research for your book and request a 20-minute interview with them. They will be blown away. Understand this clearly: No one else called them last week to be interviewed for a book. That's a hell of an honour. They won't say no, trust me on that. Then when the book comes out, send them a copy, highlight which page they are on and try to sell them a case at a discount.

7. Use Them Every Time You Have a Prospect in the Office.

Give a book to every face-to-face prospect before you start your meeting. Nothing will build your credibility and make your presentation as effective as positioning yourself as the expert author before you start talking about your products or services.

8. Give It Away to Famous People.

I published Anita Jackson's awesome book, *Rekindle The Magic In Your Relationship*, several years ago. Anita is a therapist from the UK and when her book was released, she asked me if I was going to attend her book launch. I said sure, if the Queen comes, I'll come.

Well, she must have thought I was serious because she sent a copy of her book to Her Majesty, inviting her to come to the launch. Wow!!!

A few weeks later, Anita received this letter from Buckingham Palace. Imagine that!!! The key point is the last paragraph...

> "The Queen was interested to read about the reason behind the writing of your book and thought it kind of you to send her a copy as a gift."

Royalty cannot really endorse commercial products like books, but man, this comes pretty darn close!

NOTE: Don't send your book to Queen Elizabeth – she's on to me now!

BUCKINGHAM PALACE

12th June, 2007

Dear Mrs. Jackson,

The Queen has asked me to thank you for your letter of 18th March enclosing a copy of your new book *Rekindle the Magic in your Relationship – Making Love Work*, and I apologise for the delay in replying. Due to the high volume of mail received in recent weeks, correspondence has been dealt with in strict date order.

Her Majesty was grateful for your kind invitation to attend the launch of your book on 28th March at 5pm at the Renaissance Hotel, Chancery Court, London. However, as The Queen's programme is arranged many months in advance and had already been finalised for that time, it would not have been possible for Her Majesty to accept.

I am sorry to send you a disappointing reply, but I hope that the evening was a successful and enjoyable occasion for all who took part in it.

The Queen was interested to read about the reasons behind the writing of your book and thought it kind of you to send her a copy as a gift.

Yours sincerely,

Mrs. Sonia Bonici
Senior Correspondence Officer

Mrs. Anita Jackson.

9. Hold a Book Launch Gala.

This is a celebration for doing something that most people only talk about – publishing a book! You did it, so have a party. This is a nice event, at a nice hotel and it gives you a chance to party and also sell a ton of books.

Pick a date about six to eight weeks after you get your books – you don't want to have a book launch with no books!!! (Yes, it has happened to one of my clients from Germany!) Sponsors should fund this whole affair. Approach people who want to get in front of your readers and sell them the opportunity to exhibit at your book launch, allow them to get up and say a few words. Have them pay for the wine/cheese, or the venue or the gift bags.

Invite everyone you can think of; even go after your mayor, presidents of any organizations that you belong to, all customers, prospects and, of course, the media.

Have a few people selected to give short congratulatory speeches. Have an emcee coordinate the whole thing. Call up your favourite charity and tell them that you are doing an event and would like to donate a portion of the proceeds from book sales to them. Invite them to come to your book launch party. Offer them an opportunity to show a fund-raising video and/or to say a few words to raise awareness for their cause. Then you get up last and thank everyone for being there and sell books. Tell everyone to buy two copies because a portion of the proceeds will go to that charity that just spoke.

OUR CLIENT CASE STUDY

Author : Dr. Andrea Maxim
Title : *MAXIMized Health*
Occupation : Naturepathic Doctor
Location : Toronto, Canada
Website : www.themaximmovement.com
Win : Dr. Maxim had a great book launch gala. Everything was funded by sponsors. She sold many books that night and left feeling totally excited and proud of her book and this accomplishment.

10. Don't Do Book Signings in Bookstores… It's Dumb!!!

Forget doing book signing in bookshops. Unless you are Donald Trump, it will likely backfire. Let me share my experience: I had been promoting my book, *The Millionaire Mindset*, throughout Australia and as expected, I got a call from Dymocks bookstore, the largest book chain there. They wanted to place an order for 10,000 books. I was thrilled.

But speaking with the buyer, she asked me when could I come to do a book signing in their flagship store in Perth. I said that I don't do book signings because I wasn't famous and no one knew me, and I wasn't about to set myself up for that kind of failure. She told me that she wouldn't be able to put the order in because they had a strict policy that if they placed an order for 5,000 or more books, the author HAD to do a book signing. I said too bad, I'm not doing it. She was about to hang up when I realized that she wasn't about to place the order. Needless to say, I did their stupid book signing.

It was a three-hour event. I got there and they had about 2,000 copies of my book stacked and a small card table for me to sign books on. I thought to myself, "What did you think was going to happen here today? I knew that it would flop and it did." I vowed that I would never do another one of those things again.

Well, on my way home, I was connecting in Dallas and as I ran from one gate to the other, I saw this book bloke sitting at a small card table, just like I had done in Australia the day before. There was no one around, and he just sat there like a bonehead, smiling. I had to snap this picture and as I did, our eyes met and I connected with him and felt for him; at least they gave me a balloon with "MEET THE AUTHOR" on it.

"When people have too much money, they throw launch parties, hire marketing and social-media 'experts,' buy advertising, and fly around the country on book tours. None of this will help you sell more books in a cost-effective way."

— Guy Kawasaki and Shawn Welch, authors of *APE: Author, Publisher, Entrepreneur – How to Publish a Book*

YOU CAN DO THIS!

CONCLUSION

The Most Important Thing in This Whole Book.

This will be brief...

Write your book!

These Black Card Books authors attended my Publish a Book & Grow Rich bootcamp:

GET YOUR FREE* TICKET HERE

www.publishabookandgrowrich.com/freeticket

*Not applicable in every country.

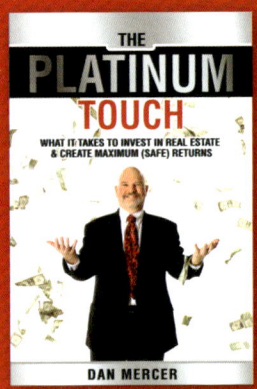
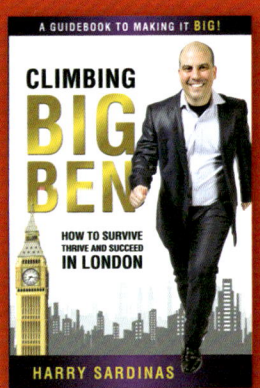

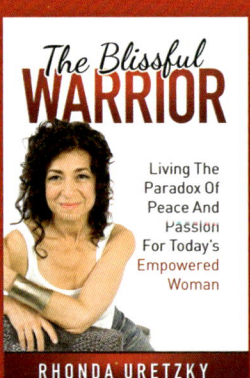
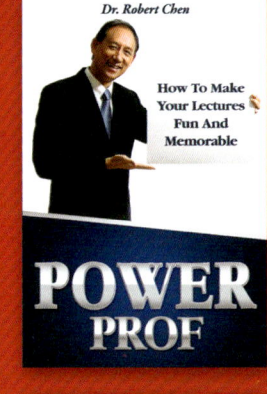
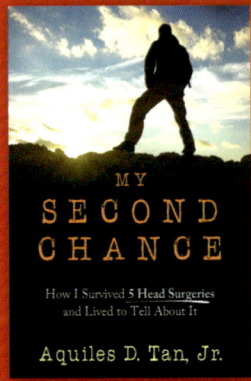
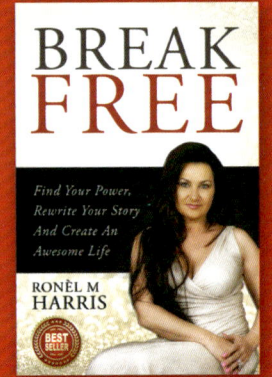
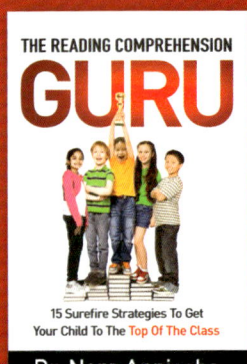
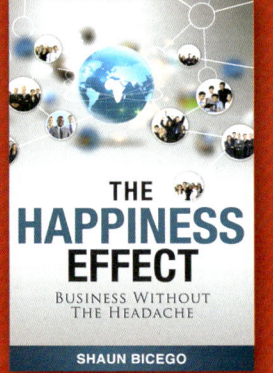

BONUS CHAPTER

by Ed Ng

Digital Empire Hack: The Shortcut to Create a Super-Charged Media Network Online

Before I start this chapter, I want to congratulate you! Whether you have written your own book or are planning to write one, it all stems from a single decision to organize your knowledge and expertise. It's structured in a way that can be easily digested by your target audience so that they may be able to learn something of value from your content. By doing so, they are more likely to perceive you as an expert in your field.

I'm here to tell you that the hardest part is now done, and that a written book, a piece of organized content, is a key that can open the door to a digital media empire. This empire has the potential to bring you continuous visitors to your website, generate new business leads and sales, attract joint venture partners and gain the attention of traditional media like television, radio, newspapers and magazines, but only if you want to. Does that interest you? If so, then please read on…

The idea of selling books by themselves to generate revenue may not be the most lucrative business model, unless you have a large following or you're a well-known brand or personality. That isn't the everyday person. If the text in a book just stays in its pages, the life of its content will just be determined by how long the book remains in circulation.

A book can either be just a sellable commodity or it can become a powerful marketing tool that can lead to the generation of other products such as seminars, workshops, group courses, coaching sessions and keynote speaking by expanding on what was outlined in the book in more depth. These are offline opportunities; however, I want to show you that a book can become a source of abundant opportunities online as well.

I want to demonstrate to you how to take the organized knowledge in a book and give it new life by translating it into different media forms such as video, audio and digital print. If the content stays inside the book, the information would only be able to reach audiences within the confines of its pages. If you leverage your content and transform them into new forms of media that's accessible online, you would be able to reach people on a global scale.

People have different learning styles and preferred ways to absorb new information. It's important to realize that these may be very different to your own. There are many different modes of learning that have been presented in various models, but I'm going to be discussing the VARK model created By Neil Fleming and his associate Dr. Colleen Mills at Lincoln University in New Zealand (1992).

Fleming was a teacher and senior inspector who oversaw over 100 high schools in New Zealand and witnessed over 9,000 classroom lessons. This experience helped him formulate a model that represented the different learning styles he observed in classrooms and this model had been adapted into early neuro-linguistic programming models (NLP) and expanded into other people's representations of learning modalities. VARK is an acronym that represents:

- **Visual** (Images, Graphics, Seeing) such as infographics, cartoons, caricatures, diagrams, flow charts, graphs and mind maps.
- **Auditory** (Musical, Aural, Listening) like podcasts, teleseminars, CDs, group coaching calls, Skype consultations and Google Hangout On Air live-streams.
- **Reading** (Text-Based, Words, Writing) for example, eBooks, Kindle books, blog articles, white papers, reports and slideshow presentations.
- **Kinesthetic**: (Physical, Tactile, Touch) which includes online practicals, how-to tutorials, demonstrations, simulations, real-life case studies, apps and interactive software.

Think about your own industry. What would be the learning style that the majority of your target market prefers? There's no point pushing content out to the public if it's in a format that is not receptive to the way your audience absorbs knowledge. They simply won't be able to digest the information to get the value out of it.

Start by focusing on creating content in the learning mode that the largest percentage of your target market favours. If you want to acquire the most market share, you should ideally produce content in all of the learning styles; that way, your content will connect with more people and access a bigger slice of the market pie. This can be a major advantage over your competitors because most businesses release content that addresses only one or two of these learning styles. The same approach can also be applied to the creation of digital products.

Leverage the content you have in your book and turn it into various digital forms. Your chapter summaries or the major points made in each chapter can become the basis of video scripts that can be delivered in front of a camera to become video content. Then you can extract the audio out of these videos and get the audio file transcribed via a transcription service or outsourced transcribers.

If you're camera shy, you can record the audio of your voice and add it to slideshow presentations that can be saved as a video file. However, you should know that showing your face on camera is a great way of building rapport with people online as it recreates the situation of meeting a person face-to-face. If you have blog entries, you can also record these as videos or audios as well.

Whatever method you choose, the end result should be three types of content formats: Video, audio and text-based transcription files. With these different forms of content, implement the following 10 steps:

1. **Schedule the videos** for upload into YouTube under your channel (make sure you add your SEO keywords, headings, and descriptions for each video). Drip feed your video content by scheduling them at a pace that is comfortable for you to maintain regularly. My recommendation is at least once a week like a television show. You can also add your videos to other video sharing sites if you want.

The VARK Learning Model

Visual — SEE!
Tip: Use Charts & Graphs
- Fast talkers
- Impatient
- Use words and phrases that evoke visual images
- See and visualise

Auditory — HEAR!
Tip: Use Verbalization
- Slow speaker
- Natural listeners
- Linear thinkers
- Prefer explanation than text
- Listen and verbalize

Reading — READ/WRITE!
Tip: Use Writing Techniques
- Prefer written text
- Emphasize text-based input and output
- Enjoy reading and writing

Kinesthetic — DO!
Tip: Demonstrate Skills
- Slow talkers
- Slow to decide
- Use all senses to engage in learning
- Prefer hands-on approaches
- Learn through trial and error

2. **Upload the audio files** to podcast sharing sites such as iTunes and Soundcloud. Once again, make sure you add in your SEO keyword optimizations, headings and descriptions, and schedule your audio uploads like a drip feed as though they were episodes on a radio show.

3. **Edit the text-based transcription files** in slideshow presentations and eBooks and save them into PDFs. You will be able to upload them to PDF sharing websites such as SlideShare, which allows people to upload and share slideshow presentations.

4. You can also **upload the content** from the text-based files into your website's blog as content articles, or offer them as guest posts on other people's websites and add a backlink to your site at the end of the article to encourage readers to visit your site after they finished reading. As a suggestion, you can also combine some of your articles together to make downloadable guides, reports, checklists or online magazines.

5. As your content posts are being released to the public, feel free to let your audience **network about it**; publish it on social media like Facebook, Twitter and LinkedIn, in your email autoresponders, weekly online newsletter, and embed the videos and podcast audio links.

6. **Add your 'digital print' materials on your website** as giveaways via opt-ins. By having an opt-in form onsite with a gift offer, you're giving something of perceived value in exchange for a visitor's contact details when they come to your website so that you may be able to contact them via emails to continue to build rapport and start a possible business relationship.

7. You may also want to look at some of your most popular pieces in your content network so far, based on audience responses in likes, shares and comments, and see if the information contained in them can be **extracted and transformed into image posts** containing tips and quotes, as well as infographics. You can then share them across your social media sites, like Pinterest, but also in your blog.

8. Over time, you'll start to notice that some of your videos, podcast episodes, blog entries and social media posts are getting more engagement than others in the form of likes, comments, shares and time spent engaging with the content. By **assessing the data,** you can identify which of your content pieces gets the most interactions with your audience and which gets the highest attention time.

9. Based on your analysis, you will discover good indications that there's interest around a few of your content pieces. You may want to **go deeper into the topic**, approach it again from a different perspective or replicate the style or format of that content into new content pieces to upload and see if you get similar responses.

10. Simply **rinse and repeat**. You now have a system to continuously produce new engaging content in different formats that will be able to inspire even more shareable content for your target market to interact with.

You can repurpose the content that you already have into many new versions of content to increase the exposure of your brand, position yourself as an expert in your field and build a traffic network leading back to your website.

The idea is to go into marketplaces of established communities where your target market hangs out, and use quality content pieces to draw them out like fish to a fishing line with a lure attached. You need to make sure that there is a way, such as a clickable link, visible URL or logo that allows the people from these traffic sources who encounter your content a way to trace back to your website to find out more about your business and what your business offers.

Not only are you creating a well-planned net to catch the attention of visitors across various social platforms, you will also be building a community, a tribe of raving fans, on each of these platforms as well.

BUILDING A COMMUNITY: THE POWER OF THE TRIBE

Like a culture of a company, creating a community in your own business is just as important as the business itself. One of the deciding factors that contributes to company valuations is the size and quality of its reach or clout, that is, its network of influence and how active and engaged is this network.

Some large organizations tap into the power of community effectively, and dedicate part of their marketing budget to create and cater for their tribes. These companies are not just focused on promoting the products and services, but also on the community that people become a part of through their purchase.

One example is Starbucks, which focuses on the lifestyle that's attached to consuming their products. This resonates with its tribe of young, trend-seekers and café enthusiasts on its social media. On their social accounts, Starbucks features the snapshot images of everyday life moments that just so happens to have a Starbucks coffee nearby.

Starbucks has also encouraged its community to post their coffee purchases on social media, as the company reposts many of their consumers' images on their own social accounts. They have created an army of content producers, rather than setting aside the time and money to make these images themselves. If your business isn't as big as Starbucks, you would still want to build a community of raving fans for the following reasons:

1. To increase the number of **active promoters** that become your "marketing team", that share, comment and like your online content, such as on your blog and social media, to reach new audiences.

2. The more interactions with your content, the more the search engines deem it as engaging. These act as **social signals** that indicate to search engine platforms, like Google and Facebook, that because there is high engagement, the content must be relevant or interesting and, therefore, should be shown to more people on the search engine results pages and news feed.

3. Your raving fans are the source of your **testimonials which add to social proof**, letting other people know how great your products and services are rather than you talking about your own business.

4. **Word of mouth is king**. Your fans are also the source of your referrals. They talk about your products and services to their own communities and introduce new business to you.

5. Your best supporters can become your **product development and product testing** team before you make your product available to the public. They can also provide feedback for updates to your existing product and services as well.

6. They can also be a source of **infinite content ideas** by involving them to contribute content and ask them what questions they still have unanswered about a certain topic your business addresses.

In biology, humans are classified as mammals and in nature, mammals like to herd together and we are no different. There's safety in numbers and we can achieve common goals faster together. Most people want to be part of a community for at least one of the following reasons:

1. **Membership**: To feel like they belong somewhere or to something.

2. **Influence**: To feel acknowledged of their existence.

3. **Integration and Fulfilment of Needs:** To contribute to something larger or greater than themselves.

4. **Shared Emotional Connection**: To seek shared emotional experiences through collective events.

5. **Responsibility:** To feel responsible for something, themselves or others in the community.

(Adapted from *David W. McMillan and David M. Chavis, Sense of Community: A Definition and Theory, 1986.*)

While every business is different, all of them require a group of people – your customers – to function. Your customers approach you with a common problem or issue they need to address and this is what connects them to your business. Here is where the concept of building a tribe comes in and how you can start thinking about implementing the above five contributing factors to create a sense of community around your business:

- Make sure you use a **customer relationship management** (CRM) software where people can opt into your database. You want to have control over the communication with your community rather than solely building your network on social media. If the social media platform makes some policy changes, or your account got hacked by someone else, then you're at risk of losing the community at a click of a finger.

- Step out of your own shoes and **slip into your audience's perspective**. What are the topics, issues and events going on in their lives at the moment? What kind of content would they be interested in looking at? What would divert their attention from all the noise in the marketplace to make them look at your business?

- **Be authentic and personable**. As humans we seek genuine connection. Just be yourself and people will naturally gravitate towards you and trust you. Large companies are taking to social media to bring more of a human side to their business; photos of CEOs are appearing on advertising and using social media to promote lifestyle rather than promote their products like Starbucks.

- **Add value** to your community consistently. Offer more value to your products and services that would exceed their expectations. Give them relevant and useful content that would benefit them, such as tips or advice in your content posting and emails. Not only will you position yourself as a trusted source but also as an authority on the subject.

- **Offer incentives and rewards** to members of your community for completing actions that grow your business, such as introducing a new referral to you, providing a testimonial or completing a feedback survey. The reward doesn't always need to have monetary value; it can simply be a public acknowledgement or promoting them on your social media.

- **Have fun**. Some businesses add game elements to add a bit of fun to their community such as collecting of points and badges for completing certain tasks. While I believe there is room for businesses to offer some element of fun or play, not every market audience is going to be interested in and respond to playing games. Know your audience well. Would they be into games being introduced to them? How can you introduce more fun into your community?

- **Get your community involved** in your business, from getting suggestions on what content you should write about on your blog, offering them opportunities for them to guest-post on your site, test run your latest products or services, and getting feedback on future product development and service updates.

Putting together a community is like building your own marketing team that you can delegate the promotion of your business to. They will freely volunteer their opinions to you simply because they feel that they have a relationship with you and believe that you have their best interest at heart. Leverage the power of your community that is more than willing to have their ideas heard and acknowledged rather than working alone.

Hopefully, now you can see that a book itself isn't where the power or the financial results lie. It's in its ability to repurpose content into other types so that it may reach even more people based on their preferred mode of communication.

By building a digital media empire, you're in control of your own media; your own 'television station' on your YouTube channel, your own 'radio station' via your podcast channel, and your own 'digital publishing house' creating your 'digital printed' materials like your guides, eBooks and online magazines.

However, having many types of content isn't enough to have your information spread, you also need to have a community: A network of active promoters to share your content out to the world and fuel your digital empire in order to attract new leads to your business and visitors to your sites, position yourself as an authority on your topic, gain media attention and joint venture partners, as well as providing feedback for new content and product ideas.

As humans, we have a tendency to complicate things, this is why I have developed a video course for you, as a reader this book, to make marketing as uncomplicated as possible to achieve effective marketing results. Simply visit **www.MarketingSynergy.com/PABGR** and put your name and email in the form to claim your access to this course for **FREE**!

In your marketing, keep it simple. Do more of what is working and less of what isn't and remember that "great business means great marketing".

Ed Ng

Ed Ng is the founder and CEO of Marketing Synergy (www.MarketingSynergy.com), a marketing company that assists and teaches business owners to implement ethical marketing and integrity selling for their business. The company markets and tests their online strategies and techniques on their own portfolio of industry leading websites. It is also an exclusive Google Partner and is Google Certified.

Ed Ng is a marketer, educator, speaker, published bestselling author and has been involved in the online marketing industry for almost a decade. He created digital marketing strategies for various international businesses such as national retail chains, e-commerce stores, local services, lead generation for highly competitive industries as well as information blogs based all over the world, including the United States, Canada and Australia.

In his working career, he's had the privilege to work with and be mentored by various influential masterminds in the mindset, business, marketing and internet worlds, combining the best of their strategies and wisdom with his own to share with his clients and students.

RESOURCES THE AUTHOR RECOMMENDS

Get 2 FREE* Tickets

Let speaking legend **GERRY ROBERT**, who has spoken to 3 million people and generated over $200 million, show you how to...

USE A BOOK AS A MARKETING TOOL

THIS IS ABOUT... Aligning yourself with **GERRY ROBERT**. Branding yourself and your business. Attracting prospects like a magnet. Building your business the Gerry Robert way. Instantly gaining EXPERT status. Generating thousands of dollars within a month. Creating massive publicity.

ATTRACTION... Making prospects come directly to you.
DISTINCTION... Being different than everyone else.
VISIBILITY... Becoming a media personality.

AUTHORITY... Creating higher profits through smart positioning.
LONGEVITY... Ensuring shelf life for your efforts.
CREDIBILITY... Branding yourself as an expert.

Attend the Publish a Book & Grow Rich bootcamp. Over 100 are conducted per year, worldwide.
www.publishabookandgrowrich.com/freeticket

*Not applicable in every country.

EARN HOW TO BUILD LIFE 2.0, THE RETIREMENT OF YOUR DREAMS.

THE DREAM RETIREMENT BOOK IS AN INSPIRATIONAL GUIDE FOR HOW TO TURN YOUR NEW LIFE INTO A FANTASTIC, FRUITFUL, AND FULFILLING EXISTENCE.

SPECIAL OFFER: FREE Copy of *The Dream Retirement* PLUS 2 BONUSES (Value £550.00)

Find out how to forecast your financial future so that you can ensure you don't run out of funds. Learn to maximise your money to ensure it is working as hard as possible for you, without taking unnecessary risks. Build an income strategy that allows you to tick off your Bucket List while you are young and healthy enough to do so. Learn to balance your time in retirement to ensure you are satisfying your basic human needs, leaving you feeling fulfilled and rewarded. Learn to boost your health and your mind, so that you stay free of disease and live out a long and energized life.

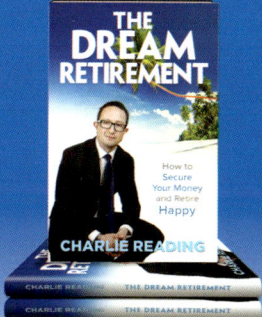

"I'm delighted to offer readers of this really terrific book an EXCLUSIVE Opportunity. Download my own book, *The Dream Retirement*, NOW for FREE here at www.dream-retirement.com/book-pabgr and I'll give you TWO additional BONUS FREE offers.

Register for *The Dream Retirement* NOW and I'll automatically send you the accompanying *Dream Retirement* Workbook, PLUS you will automatically qualify for a one-on-one FREE *Dream Retirement* Consultation with me, Charlie Reading."

Register NOW for this EXCLUSIVE Opportunity valued at over £550 here at www.dream-retirement.com/book-pabgr.

Phone Number: +44 1572 898 060 • Email Address: Hello@dream-retirement.com • Website: www.dream-retirement.com

Download a FREE Copy of *The Financial Toolbox* and Receive a DOUBLE BONUS Offer

Why do you need this FREE Book?

Jessie Christo outlines the many secrets of business finances to pay less tax, earn greater profit and save more time!

Learn the following from Financial Expert Jessie Christo:

- ☑ How to choose your all-star financial team
- ☑ Learn 4 proven ways to reduce tax on your estate
- ☑ How to avoid 14 common estate planning pitfalls
- ☑ How oversights surrounding Life, Disability and Critical Illness Insurance can destroy your business
- ☑ How to avoid 13 risks that can endanger your retirement
- ☑ How to ensure the safety of your business if your spouse or parents develop a Critical Illness
- ☑ How to create your very own Greenprint (not Blueprint)

Get your FREE downloadable copy of Jessie's book today!

Register for a FREE Downloadable Version Of The Financial Toolbox And Receive A DOUBLE BONUS For FREE (A $487 VALUE)

Jessie Christo, *The Financial Toolbox* Guru, wants you to have a **FREE** copy of his bestselling book, *The Financial Toolbox*. Register **NOW** and he'll include 2 BONUS Offers.

BONUS #1, A **FREE** copy of the accompanying *Financial Toolbox Toolkit*
PLUS BONUS #2, A **FREE** one-on-one *Financial Toolbox* Guru Consultation with the author himself, Jessie Christo.

This combined **FREE** offer is valued at over $487.

To register for your **FREE** copy of the *Financial Toolbox* and to automatically receive the **DOUBLE BONUS** offer of the toolkit and the consultation, register **NOW** at www.thefinancialtoolboxguru.com/free-financialtoolbox-book-pabgr.

PHONE NUMBER: +1 647 407 5377 • EMAIL ADDRESS: Jessie@jessiechristo.com • WEBSITE: www.thefinancialtoolboxguru.com

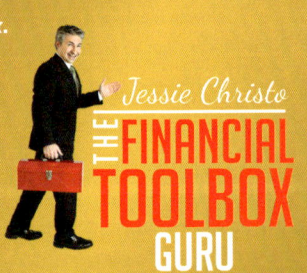

Jessie Christo THE FINANCIAL TOOLBOX GURU

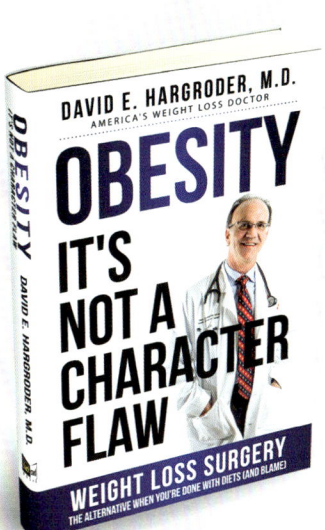

RECEIVE A FREE COPY OF DR. DAVID HARGRODER'S BOOK, *OBESITY: IT'S NOT A CHARACTER FLAW* PLUS A BONUS

Dr. Hargroder has a Special Offer for readers of this book valued at over $500.

Why Get Your FREE Copy?

David E. Hargroder, M.D. explains things in this book that most people, perhaps even your own doctor, family and friends don't know about:

- Why some seem to gain weight by simply smelling food while others eat freely without fear of weight gain.
- Why societal prejudices against those who struggle with their weight are absolutely wrong according to medical research.
- Why some people experience the "Yo-Yo" effect of dieting.
- Why some Permanent Weight Loss Solutions actually work while others don't.
- Why those who struggle with their weight can finally rejoice in knowing that Dr. Hargroder is leading the fight to educate the medical community and the world about the FACT that *Obesity is NOT a Character Flaw*!
- Learn to live again! Instead of watching life go by from the sidelines, join in the game and live life to the fullest by achieving long-term, permanent weight loss through weight loss surgery.

Download his book, **Obesity: It's Not A Character Flaw** for FREE and receive two unique BONUSES. ONE, an open invitation to Dr. Hargroder's Weekly Permanent Weight Loss Webinar. TWO, automatically qualify for a FREE Permanent Weight Loss Consultation with Dr. Hargroder himself. To start today on a journey towards permanent weight loss with America's Weight Loss Doctor, register NOW for FREE here www.blackcardbooks.leadpages.co/obesity-book-pabgr.

As Seen On...

PHONE NUMBER: +1 800 387 0514 • EMAIL ADDRESS: drh@mgb-surgery.com • WEBSITE: www.obesityisnotacharacterflaw.com

Jochen Siepmann worked in the rat race for 20 years across Europe and Asia, and then decided "ENOUGH!" He developed a wealth creation system that frankly has been around for hundreds of years but he customized it in a way where anyone with enough desire can get rich if they use this system.

"I'm pleased to offer you an Exclusive Opportunity. Buy my book, *The Property Apprentice: How To Earn While You Learn*, NOW and QUALIFY for a BONUS Property Apprentice Assessment Consult for FREE. The Consult alone is worth $500.00."

Buy a copy of Jochen's book NOW and then talk one-on-one with the author himself, Jochen Siepmann, to realize your passion for real estate investing.

Buy the book and get a FREE property consultation worth $500.00

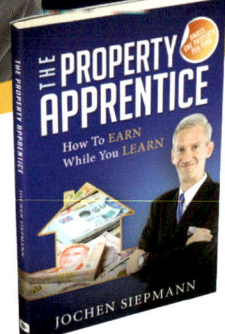

GET READY TO:
- Achieve financial success, even without lots of experience or money.
- Create a passive income that fills your bank account every month.
- Systematically plan and execute your way to financial freedom.
- Get up-to-date strategies to increasing your investment returns and understand 3 crucial mindsets every investor needs to succeed.

Buy NOW at
www.professionalpropertyinvestment.com/book-pabgr

Other details:
📞 +65 6717 0389
✉ jochen@ProfessionalPropertyInvestment.com
🌐 www.professionalpropertyinvestment.com

THE PROPERTY APPRENTICE

EARN WHILE YOU LEARN

Lillie Theresa Cawthorn
S T O R Y

"Many women tend to give away their financial power through a combination of apathy, fear and confusion. I use a straightforward, honest, simple approach to inspire women to aim higher, to regain confidence in their ability to better control their financial future."

—LILLIE CAWTHORN
Author of *The Money Factory – How Any Woman Can Make An Extra $30,000 to $100,000 Passive Income*

Lillie Cawthorn is currently the director of a Sydney-based industrial property company and has personally invested in industrial real estate in Sydney for the past 15 years.

She has real estate investment interests in Australia, France and the United States. Lillie has travelled extensively, initially investing in residential real estate across three countries, where she built and renovated homes to lease out. She is well-placed to compare the benefits of the little known industrial real estate investment opportunity to the more commonly known residential real estate investment domain.

Currently residing in Sydney, she has industrial property investment interests in small unit factories, larger conventional factories and warehouses and industrial property trusts.

Lillie is the author of *The Money Factory – How Any Woman Can Earn An Extra $30,000 To $100,000 Passive Income*.

She is passionate about inspiring women to take control of their financial future. Lillie holds workshops and seminars for select groups of women who would like to learn how to own their own money factory.

Reclaim Your Power: How Money Factory Investing Generates Independence & Wealth

Take Back Your Power
We are all capable of achieving more in life, but finding the inner strength and encouragement can be daunting. Lillie shares her motivating story of overcoming obstacles and finding the courage to step out of her comfort zone to write her book, *The Money Factory*, and gain recognition within the property industry.

Money Matters
These money-handling strategies will show you how thoughts and habits are affecting your finances. Whether you are just starting to save for your first investment deposit or are ready to fund an investment, implementing these tips and tricks will fast-track you to investment success.

Find the Right People
Do you find negotiating unfamiliar territory daunting? Perhaps you are unsure how to find the right people to help you take the next step towards securing your investment goal. Do you feel intimidated by business 'jargon'? You are not alone! Learn how to negotiate the 'BS' in the business world and find the right people to help you move toward your investment goal.

By the End of This Presentation You Will:
1. Know how to identify the primary areas where you allow your money to slip away.
2. Learn how to listen to your internal 'BS meter' in the business world.
3. Overcome fears that hold you back from earning 'set it and forget it' extra income.
4. Feel confident that you can control your financial future.
5. Discover 7 Power Tips for investing in industrial real estate.

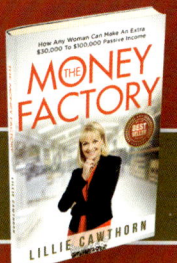

Get Your FREE Digital Copy of *The Money Factory* and FREE Industrial Property Guide
here at www.moneyfactoryinvesting.com/book-pabgr

For more information on dates/times for the *Reclaim Your Your Power* seminars, contact **LILLIE THERESA CAWTHORN**
PHONE NUMBER: +61 422 342 351 • EMAIL ADDRESS: info@themoneyfactory.com.au • WEBSITE: www.WomenReclaimingPower.com

YOU TOO CAN SUCCEED!!!

Success Fundamentals Vol. II

Written by an award-winning author, mentor and coach, Adv. Mary Bosiu. She was born and bred in a tiny village (not a city or town) located in a rural community in the Mountain Kingdom of Lesotho. She transcended the usual and normal, as she passionately pursued her dream. What is that dream? To inspire people into success! *Success Fundamentals Vol. II* is one of her latest achievements. Grab yourself a copy. In this book you will learn how to:

- Be a prophet of a wonderful and success-filled life that you deserve.
- Shut your mind to the mental noise generated by chronic worry and destructive fear.
- Give time the time to heal you with respect to the pain over which you have no control.
- Avoid tying your self-worth to what other people think or say about you.
- And lots, lots more…

Emotional Maturity: A Door to Success!!!!!!

Speaking & Training Themes:

Academic accolades need to be paired up with other skills that give meaning to life, skills that build up emotional maturity, integrity, service excellence and inner peace. If you want your employees to have such skills, look no further! Mary can brilliantly hand-hold them. These are some of the themes for her training and speaking engagements:

- "Jump Off the Blame Treadmill"
- "Fame Without Shame is a Flame"
- "Setbacks are Setups for you to Step Up"
- "Excel: Money Loves Quality"
- "Master Emotional Mastery"
- And any other customer-tailored programs…

Do this Now: Download a **FREE** *Report on…*

How you can view setbacks as "stairs" to propel you into action – to keep on keeping on. Remember: You are not a failure. You too can succeed!

Visit her at www.marybosiu.com

I Can Show You How To Transform Your Life

Do you feel there must be more to life?

Do you want to feel happier and less stressed?

Do you want to change your life for the better?

If you answer yes to any of these questions, then I can help you.

Sign up for my email series '**Twenty Ways To Transform Your Life**' and I'll reveal the secrets my clients pay to hear – and send them straight to your inbox for FREE. When you sign up, you also get a **FREE copy** of my latest book – Living The Extraordinary Life: The 8-Step Practical Plan, which normally sells for US$32.

YOU WILL DISCOVER HOW TO:

- ✓ Set realistic goals you can and will achieve
- ✓ Find time in your busy life to focus on you
- ✓ Beat procrastination to get more done in less time

And much, much more!

Simply go to **www.extraordinarylife.co/Gerry** and enter your details.

Liesha Eggink
Transformational Coach

As a transformational coach, it's my job to understand people's problems and transform their lives – people just like you. I combine life coaching skills with my experience as a corporate trainer, which has led major companies such as Aviva, Unilever, Burberry and the Rothschild Group to employ me to support and train their staff.

You can now get my help for FREE.
Simply visit my site to start living the life you deserve.

Act now, while this is on your mind.
Just go to www.extraordinarylife.co/Gerry and download my book for FREE.

See what it takes to reach the stars!

There is a fine line between determination and obstinacy. Losing the power to fight on? Learn and follow Sandra's 6-step strategy and see how you can achieve your goals easily today!

 Scan the QR code now for a FREE digital book by Sandra and a special discount on her business tools and systems to kick-start your own business today.

SANDRA YEOW
AUTHOR | ENTREPRENEUR | BUSINESS & IT CONSULTANT

Email Address: contact@sandrayeow.com
Phone Number: +65 3152 2888
Website: www.obstinacypower.com

80% OF YOUR SALES COME FROM 20% OF YOUR CUSTOMERS

Businesses are constantly chasing new customers: Building relationships with your existing customer base must be a priority.

In *Your Customer Is King*, Stephen McCullagh looks at how to build relationships with your customers to ensure their loyalty, as well as develop strategies to increase revenue through your existing customer base. He also uncovers techniques to strengthen a new customer base without the associated traditional costs.

- Connect with your customers
- Use technology to your advantage at low cost
- Increase revenue
- Retain more customers

Register for your copy now at **www.customer-king.com/pabgr** and receive a:

- FREE customer care worksheet.
- FREE weekly e-zine with tips and strategies on how to develop relationships with your customers.

The Express Money Train™

ROWENA HAMILTON

Buy the book or get a downloadable version from

www.expressmoneytrain.com

Bonus Chapter! How to Travel for FREE

Looking for a 1st Class Life for you and your family?

Life is like a long distance train ride... Follow our tracks to build your own wealth and propel yourself to a better station in life.

Don't miss the chapter on... The Kids' Express Money Train.

For less than a cup of coffee a day... let me show you the simple formula that will set your young children up for life!

No shiny Harvard degrees needed... "If we can do it... you can too!"

"Some people earn a fortune in their lives and have very little to show for it. We started with very little and built a fortune in ours... you can too! You can choose to live a mean life... OR Learn to E-X-P-A-N-D your MEANS to fit the LIFE you CHOOSE!"

Want to change your life? Discover how to
OVERCOME ANYTHING!

Want to perform at your highest level? Seeking a massive shift to transform your business or personal life for lifelong success? Meet international speaker and acclaimed author, S.T. Wilkinson.

Whether you're facing a major challenge or critical crossroad, Wilkinson's coaching expertise and unique methodologies in decision making and crisis intervention will help you gain:

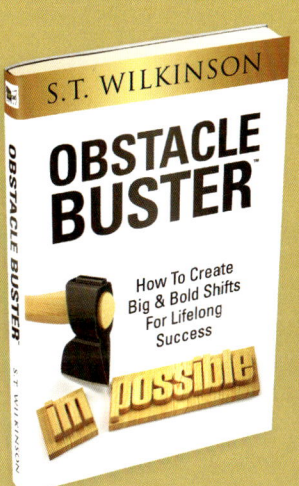

INSTANT CLARITY
To Know What You Want

CONFIDENT DIRECTION
To Go After What You Want

TRUE PURPOSE
To Get What You Want

Become an expert "Obstacle Buster™" today! Eliminate blocks and handle any challenges you face to create massive success. Move forward proactively and passionately to accelerate reaching your goals. Finally win the freedom and lifestyle you know you deserve!

Claim Your FREE Life-Changing Gift Now At:

www.authorstwilkinson.com
Email Address: **info@authorstwilkinson.com**

BECOME THE ABSOLUTE BEST VERSION OF YOU!

Author of *TRIUMPH Through TRAGEDY. Heaven-Sent Guide On BECOMING The BEST YOU When Life Hurts The Most.*

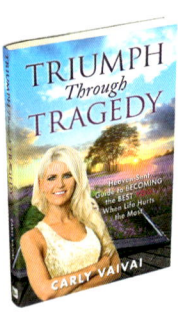

With complete customisation & high quality support, Carly will help you.

- Bring your sexy back
- Attain peak performance
- Increase your confidence
- Stop feeling sick & tired
- Experience optimum health & vitality
- Lose body fat whilst enjoying your lifestyle
- Transform your physique, change your life
- Fast track your results & be held accountable
- Stay motivated & feel supported
- Get results that last a lifetime

"The greatest gift you can give to others is a HAPPY & HEALTHY YOU"

For the results you've always wanted, scan the QR code now or visit **www.carlyvaivai.com** today to receive your **FREE** confidential **55 minute 'No fuss, fast result'** consultation. (online coaching available).

Committed to empowering, transforming & changing lives...

Carly Vaivai

International Speaker
Fitness & Nutrition Specialist
Personal Performance Coach
Business Mentor & Entrepreneur
Pastoral Care & Grief Consultant

Contact

Australian office: +61 (0)2 8080 8213
American office: +1 800 956 4080 (toll free)
London office: +44 (0)20 3905 2822
Email Address: carly@carlyvaivai.com
Web: www.carlyvaivai.com

Proudly supports the Herbalife Family Foundation (H.F.F). "Helping Children Around The World"

Waste Connects

JOIN THE REVOLUTION,
BECOME THE SOLUTION.

Everywhere we look these days, there is nothing but pain! Social demand for change! The need for new ideas to solve global problems. Our world needs independent thinking and strong leadership! And yet we all have so much social and internal pressure to be like everyone else and not STAND OUT!

GET OUT OF THE BOX! Start living NOW! Is about one person's journey towards 'independent thinking.'

Get a FREE consultation or additional resources and digital books on Environment Management through waste control. Go to **www.JenniferHolmes.online.**

JENNIFER HOLMES
CEO | Author | Speaker

Email Address: **Jennifer@WasteConnects.com**
Phone Number: **(Australia) +61 1300 258 580**
Website: **www.JenniferHolmes.online**

How to Become a Highly-Paid and Sought-After
CELEBRITY
in Your Industry in 60 Days from Podcasts

If you are struggling to get your name out there or get traction, text "celebrity" to 31996 for your FREE copy*!

Here's just a few of the things you'll learn:

- How to build 6 revenue streams from the monetization of your show
- How to create your own recording studio for less than $300
- How to build an engaged and passionate community of fans
- Land AMAZING celebrity guests you dream of talking to on your show
- Create an AWESOME, non-boring show people can't stop listening to
- How to interview like a rock star even if your major is not journalism

Testimonial

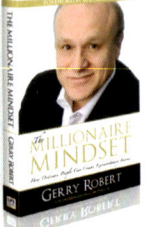

"With over 1+ billion downloads of podcast shows on iTunes, *Awaken The Celebrity Within* holds the keys to reach potentially millions of engaged and targeted people quickly and easily, build a community and leverage it to generate more income! So drop what you are doing and read it."

GERRY ROBERT, international bestselling author of *The Millionaire Mindset*

About Author Michael Nguyen

Michael Nguyen is the leading authority on creating podcast shows to help you become a highly-paid celebrity. He is the CEO and publisher of *Asian Success Magazine*, host of the *Asian Success Show* and *Born To Be Speaker Show*, and a professional public speaker.

Text "celebrity" to 31996 for your FREE Copy*! or visit www.awakenthecelebritywithin.com.

*Standard message and data rates may apply.

Sanity 365

Donate a Book per Month & the Author Will Give It Away on Your Behalf to People Who Are Hurting

The 100,000 Book Giveaway Program

GIVE A BOOK A MONTH DIRECTLY TO A HURTING PERSON

THE OUR HOUSE PROGRAM

This unique fundraising and inspiring program will put a book that you donate every month directly into the hands of a hurting person. It will provide practical help and solutions and give them hope that they can recover.

HOW DOES IT WORK?

1. You will sign up to donate one copy of Norm's groundbreaking book *Sanity 365* per month. Of course, you can cancel at any time.

Canadian residents can receive a tax deductible receipt.

2. Norm and the Our House team will take that book to the streets of Vancouver and other major cities and put it (YOUR BOOK) directly into the hands of a hurting person. Your first name will be inscribed along with Norm's autograph on the inside of the book.

3. They will report to you periodically who has received your kindhearted gifts. Of course, we want to respect everyone's privacy.

Our House is a program for men and women who have addictions and who often are homeless. The participants live together as a family in a residential neighbourhood.

As in any family, they share the tasks of daily life – cooking, house cleaning and maintenance and personal care.

But, in addition, they must meet each morning as a group to talk about their problems and their experiences of living with addiction

The program assists residents towards recovery and helps them "re-socialize" into mainstream society. The program is based on self-help; it employs no professional staff.

FOR MORE INFORMATION, Please Contact:
The House Manager **Gerry Oake**
Phone Number: **+1 604 594 1168** | Email Address: **info@sanity365.com**

What follows are real-world examples of people who have attended my world-famous Publish a Book & Grow Rich bootcamp.

Grab your FREE* ticket now!

www.publishabookandgrowrich.com/freeticket

*Not applicable in every country.

TESTIMONIALS

Kim Speed

Author of *Branding on a Shoestring*
Branding and Marketing

Email: kspeed@purplemooncreative.com
Website: www.purplemooncreative.com
Visit my website to receive a FREE brand strategy session.

What is your Primary Objective?
I want my book to help me become known as a small business brand expert and help me get speaking engagements.

What has been your biggest win?
I've already been approached to speak at small business conferences and seminars and I've made new connections and partnerships just by presenting myself as an author. My business has grown in the few months I've been working with Gerry and Black Card Books.

What has been your experience working with Gerry Robert?
Gerry provides encouragement and pushes you to get going. He provides tools and advice that are useful and easily implemented. Even as a marketer I've found that Gerry provides an amazing amount of information to help fund and market not only the book but also my business. This has been truly invaluable to me.

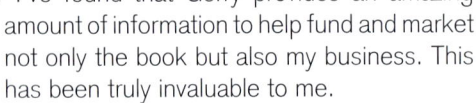
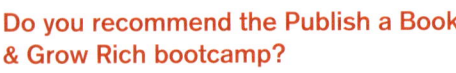

Do you recommend the Publish a Book & Grow Rich bootcamp?
This is one of the most powerful seminars ever.

Lillie Cawthorn

Author of *The Money Factory*
Author, Director, Investor, Speaker

Email: lillietc3@gmail.com
Website: www.moneyfactoryinvesting.com
Visit my website to receive a FREE copy of my book.

What is your Primary Objective?
My objective is to show women how I have built an investment portfolio of industrial properties returning passive income, all whilst working from home.

What has been your biggest win?
In the first six weeks, I sold $28,500 worth of sponsor presales. An unexpected spinoff was that I became a motivational speaker for women and got massive media attention, including TV and radio appearances.

What has been your experience working with Gerry Robert?
The absolutely first-class supportive, nurturing, encouraging, mentoring and educating care provided by Gerry and Black Card Books throughout the writing, production and launch of the book surpassed all expectations. Gerry and the team enabled me to do it all in only seven months.

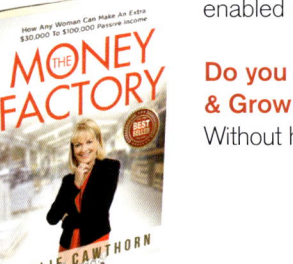

Do you recommend the Publish a Book & Grow Rich bootcamp?
Without hesitation. Get yourself to a bootcamp.

Tan Choon Kiang

Author of *Life Makeover*
International Speaker, Trainer

Email: tanck98@icloud.com
Website: www.TanChoonKiang.com
Visit my website to receive a FREE ticket to my two-hour "Aligning Your Subconscious" seminar.

What is your Primary Objective?
To enhance my credibility as an international trainer and speaker. To effectively promote my speaking engagements and my seminars.

What has been your biggest win?
My enhanced credibility as an author has helped my energy-healing seminar, "Unleash Your Inner Qi", penetrate the Japanese market, and opened up the huge potential for making it to many more countries in the near future.

What has been your experience working with Gerry Robert?
When you work with Gerry, you're really working with a team of capable, dedicated people who can and will turn your dreams in to reality. If you want to get your book done, this is the team! The best team I have ever worked with. They're incredibly fun and, more importantly, they're highly effective!

Do you recommend the Publish a Book & Grow Rich bootcamp?
Yes, but don't take my word for it go and see for yourself.

Rich Clouse

Author of *Rich Dentist Poor Dentist*
Salesman

Email: rich@gcellc.com
Website: www.gcellc.com
Visit my website to receive a FREE copy of the book.

What is your Primary Objective?
I want to provide a marketing vehicle to attract dentists to become my clients. I also want to donate books to dental charities and dental school students.

What has been your biggest win?
A client who read the book sent it to his son who is in dental school. He read it in one day and liked it so much he gave it to one of his professors the next day to read.

What has been your experience working with Gerry Robert?
Black Card Books has provided me with much more support than I expected and surprised me by making far more additions to my book than I ever thought they would.

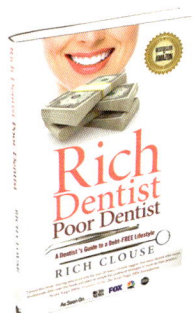

Do you recommend the Publish a Book & Grow Rich bootcamp?
This workshop is jam-packed with solid actionable content.

Ahmad-Shah Duranai

Author of *The Leadership Zone*
Leadership and Communications Coach, Trainer, Speaker

Email: asdk@sympatico.ca
Website: www.duranet.ca
To receive a FREE copy of my book, click www.theleadershipzone31.com.

What is your Primary Objective?
My objective for the book is to expand my authority and credibility as a Leadership and Communications Coach, and to get my name out in front of top corporate executives.

What has been your biggest win?
My biggest win was being flown to Africa by an international consulting firm to train United Nations staff. Later, I was flown to the United Arab Emirates to do a workshop with zone managers of a bank.

What has been your experience working with Gerry Robert?
Gerry Robert is a superb teacher, mentor and marketer when it comes to books and publicity. I'm grateful for his teaching and mentorship, and for all the support his dedicated team has given me to publish my book.

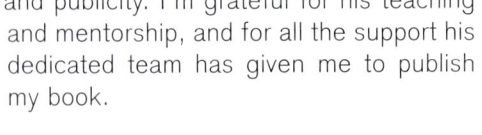

Do you recommend the Publish a Book & Grow Rich bootcamp?
I've been to it for almost 10 times. So YES, I give it two thumbs up.

Alex Figueroa

Author of *ASSESS THIS!*
Teacher

Email: alexfig09@yahoo.com
Website: www.powerofintrospection.com/FREE
Visit my website to get a FREE downloadable copy of *Assess This!*

What is your Primary Objective?
I want the book to bring in revenue, provide me with speaking engagements and expand my opportunities to run seminars, teach workshops, lead bootcamps and offer coaching and training development courses.

What has been your biggest win?
I became a bestselling author in North America; I was recognised as Teacher of the Year 2015 by my local VFW (Veterans of Foreign Wars) post. I was selected as principle leadership advisor for a leadership and engineering academy in my local school district. And I received a letter of appreciation from the former First Lady, Mrs. Michelle Obama, for my gifting the First Family a signed copy of my book, *Assess This!*

What has been your experience working with Gerry Robert?
Working with Gerry Robert and the team at Black Card Books has been fabulous. Gerry is a wonderful mentor who loves and cares for

all his authors and employees. He's developed first-class training and support systems that embody his beliefs and core values. Most importantly, Gerry Robert and his team have great passion and unquestionable integrity.

Do you recommend the Publish a Book & Grow Rich bootcamp?
I've attended tons of courses. This is one of the most helpful ever. Worth every penny!

Allan made the decision to move from a comfortable, safe corporate office to sharing a desk with three others in a Dealership. Life in corporate was simply not challenging enough, and he was frustrated having to tell everyone how to do their jobs when he hadn't done it himself. Thus, he left his Corporate management role to gain an understanding of retail from the ground up. Rather than moving horizontally, to another management role within a Dealership, he wanted to start at the bottom and work his way up. He did just that, moving from salesman to general sales manager of the biggest Lexus dealership in Australia, a mission he accomplished in just three years, spending over five years in the Dealership.

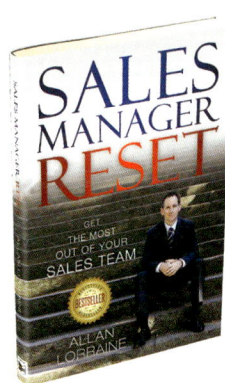

Learn How To...

- Learn how to manage staff and create a great team.
- Learn about enquiry conversion and capture.
- Take advantage of personality selling/matching.
- Improve your gross profit.
- Sell to different cultures.
- Manage your peers for mutual success.

FREE OFFER
Full Downloadable book + **FREE** Career Development Self-Assessment & Personal Consultation with the Author. (Over $300 value)
www.salesmanagerreset.com

Phone Number: **+61 408 553 453**
Email Address: **allan@biresults.com.au**
Website: **www.BiResults.com.au**

Benjamin Foo

Author of *iPOSSIBLE*®!
Author, Speaker-Coach, Entrepreneur, Investor

Email: benjaminfoo@iPossible-International.com
Website: www.iPossible-International.com
Visit my website to receive your FREE *iPOSSIBLE*® Guidebook.

What is your Primary Objective?
To build my credibility and create a sustainable reputation as an author, speaker and coach. I want to be known as an authority who inspires individuals and helps executives and business owners change their organizational destinies.

What has been your biggest win?
I'm proud to have published a powerful book that gives real hope and practical advice that changes the destinies of individuals, teams and organizations.

What has been your experience working with Gerry Robert?
I'd been planning to write a book for decades. Then I met Gerry Robert at his exciting workshop packed with all the know-how an author needs. He was the catalyst I needed.

In five months, defying impossible odds, *iPOSSIBLE*® was published on schedule. I couldn't have done it without the awesome support of the Black Card Books team!

Do you recommend the Publish a Book & Grow Rich bootcamp?
Just go. You'll see!!!

Patsy Chia

Author of *Burden No More*
Author, Speaker, Mentor

Email: patsygoh188@gmail.com
Website: www.patsychia.com
Visit www.patsychia.com/consultation to get a FREE consultation.

What has been your biggest win?
Since becoming an author, my life has changed. I'm now more positive and confident when I meet challenges in my life. Now I use them to grow and improve.

What has been your experience working with Gerry Robert?
Gerry Robert is a wonderful publisher who won't hesitate to push you to your limit. I've learned a lot working with Gerry. His program opened my eyes to a whole new beginning for me. It's true that being an author gives you credibility. Gerry and his team are just awesome.

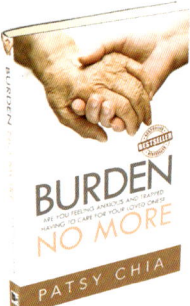

Do you recommend the Publish a Book & Grow Rich bootcamp?
It was funny, fast, content-rich, practical, easy to follow and, best of all, real. No hype or motivational psychobabble.

Christine Louis de Canonville

Author of *THE THREE FACES OF EVIL*
Psychotherapist

Email: cldec@hotmail.com
Website: www.narcissisticbehavior.net/book
Visit my website to receive a FREE Complete Article Collection on Narcissistic Behaviour.

What is your Primary Objective?
To position myself as an authority of the field of Psychopathy, an expert on Narcissistic Victim Syndrome, and help me bring my message to a broader audience. I want it to give me credibility for the purpose of educating other professionals, as well as generate multiple income streams I can leverage when I retire from being a psychotherapist.

What has been your biggest win?
For me it was getting the backing of the two largest accreditation boards in my field. They invited me to speak at a major conference, which was a huge honour indeed.

What has been your experience working with Gerry Robert?
It's been a most positive experience. Eighteen months ago, becoming an author was just a dream. Gerry and the Black Card Books team have been the encouraging force behind my success. They've helped me reach amazing heights in a very short time.

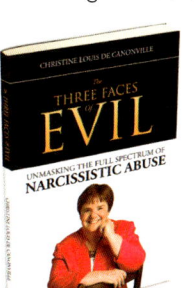

Do you recommend the Publish a Book & Grow Rich bootcamp?
Since attending the bootcamp, my world has exploded in the best possible way. Gerry's coaching and advice enabled me to the highest level.

David McCammon

Author of *IMAGE POWER*
Photographer, Educator, Author, Speaker, Consultant

Email: david@davidmcphoto.com
Website: www.davidmcphoto.com
Visit my website to receive a FREE offer.

What is your Primary Objective?
My primary objective is to help photographers develop an understanding of their value and grow their business.

What has been your biggest win?
My biggest win since joining BCB has been rebooting my own self-confidence and connecting with people who are equally passionate about photography and committed to the ongoing commercial success of up-and-coming photographers!

What has been your experience working with Gerry Robert?
Gerry Robert's word is impeccable. When he says he helps ordinary people do extraordinary things he means it and follows through. His team is first class. Gerry Robert is the real deal. He helps people everywhere accomplish what they never thought they could. The books he publishes are amazing!

Do you recommend the Publish a Book & Grow Rich bootcamp?
I highly recommend the Publish a Book & Grow Rich Bootcamp. Gerry and his team are excellent at what they do. They are consistently supportive and highly motivational.

Jan Miller, Marg and Bob MacLean

Authors of *The E-Syndrome*
Success Facilitators

Email: info@newbisystem.com
Website: bcboffer.members.newbisystem.com
Visit our website to receive FREE access to NEWBI Nation for three months and a coaching evaluation session.

What is your Primary Objective?
Our primary objective is to gain credibility by being authors. By leveraging this credibility, we're attracting highly-motivated entrepreneurs to the NEWBI Nation, our premiere community.

What has been your biggest win?
Our book, even before it was published, cemented our reputation as serious business people. Its success led to the expansion of our joint-venture opportunities as well as multiple streams of income within NEWBI Nation and for our members.

What has been your experience working with Gerry Robert?
After one meeting with Gerry, we transformed our business' mission and purpose. His guidance solidified our thinking and allowed us to leverage our skills and assets to their best advantage. Working with the Black Card Books team was a dream.

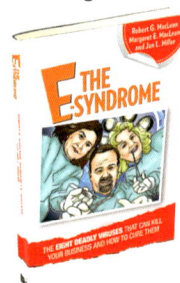

Do you recommend the Publish a Book & Grow Rich bootcamp?
We do seminars and only wish we can attain this level of education. Just GO!

Chris Dyson

Author of *Target Practice*
Author, Professional (Ice Hockey) Goalie Consultant and Coach

Email: info@authorchrisdyson.com,
info@puckstoppers.com
Website: www.puckstoppers.com,
www.authorchrisdyson.com
Visit my website to receive a FREE personal consulting or coaching session.

What is your Primary Objective?
I want my book to build my status as a coach and open new doors that will allow me to open a new web-based business for coaches. I also want to develop a coaching certification process for North America.

What has been your biggest win?
The book has helped create new relationships and garner exposure that wouldn't have been possible without it.

What has been your experience working with Gerry Robert?
Gerry Robert is an incredible wealth of information and knowledge combined with a wonderful personality. He's clearly committed to helping others achieve their dreams and obviously loves what he does. Meeting and working with Gerry has been an incredible experience.

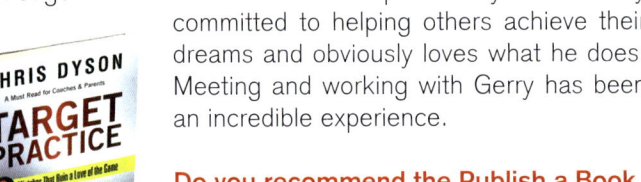

Do you recommend the Publish a Book & Grow Rich bootcamp?
I cannot recommend this program enough.

Meow Ling Ng

Co-Author of *Life Sucks!*
IT Senior Manager

Email: meowling@magTIM.com
Website: www.lifesucksbooks.com
Visit www.lifesucksbooks.com/all-about-the-mind for a FREE copy of the mind recipe book, *All About The Mind.*

What is your Primary Objective?
I want to gain recognition, increase my credibility and quit my current job!

What has been your biggest win?
I've made a complete, 360-degree turnaround in my perspective on life. I know my true purpose. My biggest win has been becoming an author, and doing it for my two darling daughters to see.

What has been your experience working with Gerry Robert?
Great! Despite his busy schedule, Gerry makes sure that all the authors will be able to complete and publish their books.

Do you recommend the Publish a Book & Grow Rich bootcamp?
Two days in the PABGR bootcamp has changed and benefited our entire lives. It is the most valuable knowledge we have ever gained!

Anm Pek

Author of *The Secret Code: Is It For Real?*

Email: anm@anmpek.com
Website: www.gameoflifeacademy.com/metaphysics
Visit my website to discover your
#1 Power and get FREE access to Character Metaprofiling Tools.

What is your Primary Objective?
To attract and increase business sales and opportunities.

What has been your biggest win?
This process has totally changed how I market myself and my business. It's so easy now. Prospects are attracted to me and want to purchase my products and services.

What has been your experience working with Gerry Robert?
Gerry made it possible for me to become a published author, and gave me a brand-new approach in both my personal and business branding.

Do you recommend the Publish a Book & Grow Rich bootcamp?
If you want to be the best, attend the best, learn from the best and let me assure you when it comes to marketing, publishing and wealth, this course is the best.

Anna Shilina

Author of *The Business Tango*
Author, Speaker, Coach

Email: connectwith@authorannashilina.com
Website: www.authorannashilina.com
Visit my website to receive a FREE download of my book.

What is your Primary Objective?
To establish and increase my credibility and grow my readership and community. To attract coaching clients and get speaking engagements.

What has been your biggest win?
My biggest win was being offered to speak on an international speaker's stage at a prestigious event. The book has also provided me the platform I needed to start a YouTube channel and share my message like never before.

What has been your experience working with Gerry Robert?
Meeting Gerry changed my life. Without him, I would never have found the courage to write my book, much less had access to a system to publish it. Gerry believed my story could change lives. His belief took me to unprecedented heights in my personal development and my professional capacity.

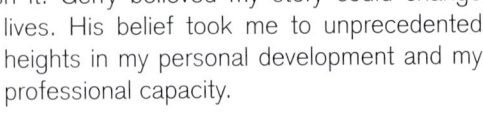

Do you recommend the Publish a Book & Grow Rich bootcamp?
I can't imagine where my life and my business would be today if I had not attended this bootcamp. I loved it.

Rajiv D. Talreja

Author of *LEAD or BLEED*
Author, Speaker, Business Coach

Email: rajiv@quantumleap.co.in
Website: www.rajivtalreja.com
Email me to receive access to my FREE business breakthrough webinar.

What is your Primary Objective?
To generate a substantial lead list for business coaching filled with entrepreneurs eager to scale up their business.

What has been your biggest win?
I've signed up as a speaker with India's largest seminar organizer to promote my programs.

What has been your experience working with Gerry Robert?
Gerry and his team at Black Card Books are the Rolls-Royce of publishing. Gerry is a master of the business and gives you practical and powerful strategies that can change your trajectory. Working with Black Card Books has been a life-changing experience for me.

Do you recommend the Publish a Book & Grow Rich bootcamp?
I'm so fortunate this seminar came to India. I tell everyone about it. It's life-changing.

Scott Tsui

Author of *Lonely No More*
Author, Relationship Coach

Email: scott.tsui@gmail.com
Website: www.scotttsui.com
Send an email to scotttsui@lonelynomorebook.com and get your FREE access to Gay Men Relationship Blueprint Online Course for every purchase of my book.

What is your Primary Objective?
I want my book to be the primary marketing tool I use to promote my future online courses.

What has been your biggest win?
The book helped me gain recognition and get established as an authority in my area of expertise.

What has been your experience working with Gerry Robert?
Excellent. Gerry provides detailed information and step-by-step strategies on how to be successful as an author and expert.

Do you recommend the Publish a Book & Grow Rich bootcamp?
I've paid hundreds of thousands to attend seminars and bootcamps. I can say that I was shocked at the value this one brought to me and my business. Everyone at the course absolutely loved it, and so did I.

Michelle Watson

Author of *Overcome And Rise Above*
Author, Coach, Speaker

Email: michellewatson@breakfreemw.com
Website: www.break-freeforever.com
Visit my website to receive a FREE downloadable copy of my book.

What is your Primary Objective?
To establish my authority and credibility as an author, coach and speaker. To open doors of opportunity and position me as an expert in my field.

What has been your biggest win?
My biggest win by far is starting my own business, which the book made possible because it gave me the authority and presence I needed to make it all happen. I've also gained a lot of television and radio publicity, and I've received an offer to host my own 30-minute radio show.

What has been your experience working with Gerry Robert?
Phenomenal experience. The greatest of my life. I enjoy the fact that I have a mentor who is open, genuine and passionate about taking ordinary people and turning them into extraordinary people by giving them the ability to not only be outstanding but also to stand out. I wish I'd met him earlier in my life.

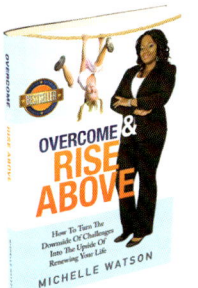

Do you recommend the Publish a Book & Grow Rich bootcamp?
Well, the proof is in the pudding. I'm a published author.

KEVIN JUDGE is an author, speaker, coach and consultant. Described as forward-thinking, pragmatic and trustworthy, Kevin works with leaders and organizations to produce extraordinary results and transform impossible futures into reality. His goal is to help build a world in which the vast majority of people and organizations prosper from winning manager-employee relationships. To achieve this goal, he is leading a movement to emphasize the criticality of strong leadership.

Learn How To...

- Finally eliminate the trail of financial and interpersonal distress a bad boss creates, without firing that boss.
- Help bad bosses see the damage, alter their behavior and develop effective strategies to change their approach.
- Create a path to success and greater results for employees, leaders and the company.

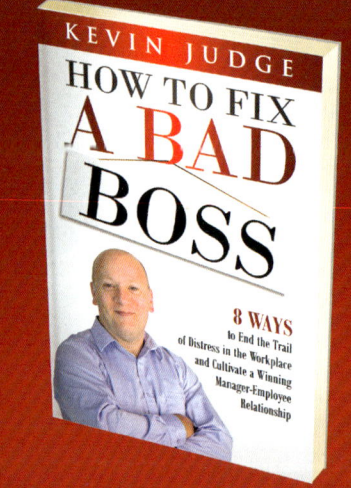

Scan the QR code now for a **FREE** one-on-one situation assessment with the author. ($300 value)
www.fixabadboss.com/book

Phone Number: +1 613 668 9905
Website: www.FixaBadBoss.com
Email Address: judge@fixabadboss.com

Jack H. M. Wong

Author of *Cracking The Entrepreneur Code*
Consultant, International Speaker

Email: jack@jackhmwong.com
Website: www.CrackingEntrepreneurCodeBook.com
Email me to receive a FREE 30-minute online business strategy consultation.

What is your Primary Objective?
My goal for this book is to help me build my credibility and become an authority on the topic of entrepreneurship. I'd have to say that as a business consultant and an international speaker, credibility is mission-critical.

What has been your biggest win?
I've travelled to four different continents and spoken on stage with Gerry and other celebrities in Singapore, Malaysia and Japan. I was one of the few speakers from Singapore invited to speak in South Africa.

What has been your experience working with Gerry Robert?
Gerry is phenomenal because of his rich experience in the publishing and speaking industries. Everyone in the Black Card Books team is supportive and encouraging. I'm happy to be part of the family!

Do you recommend the Publish a Book & Grow Rich bootcamp?
Make time and he'll help you crack the code to wealth and marketing.

Adeline Heng

Author of *Doing Good And Doing Well*
Author, Speaker, Consultant

Email: adelineheng@gmail.com
Website: www.doinggooddoingwell31.com
Visit my website to receive a FREE copy of my book.

What is your Primary Objective?
To open doors and grow my client list. It's all about lead generation.

What has been your biggest win?
Getting over the obstacles that kept me from speaking. I didn't crave being on stage. Today, speaking on stage is almost second nature to me. Would not have been possible without *Publish a Book & Grow Rich!*

What has been your experience working with Gerry Robert?
The Black Card Books team has been most helpful, wonderful and patient. Even when I was too busy to return their messages in a timely manner, they kept encouraging me to press on, and it worked. A really positive team.

Do you recommend the Publish a Book & Grow Rich bootcamp?
Everyone in Singapore loves Gerry and this seminar. Thousands here have attended and have been inspired, educated and trained to get their books done. You can, too.

Andreea Mihalcea

Author of *Speed Selling*
Author, Sales Coach, Transformational Speaker

Email: deeamihalcea@gmail.com
Website: www.andreeamihalcea.com
Visit my website to receive a FREE copy of my book and FREE access to my Speed Selling webinars.

What is your Primary Objective?
My book will position me as a high-profile speaker and sales coach, increase my number of high-paying and high-quality customers and land me top-shelf speaking engagements.

What has been your biggest win?
My income quadrupled in the first month of introducing myself as an upcoming book author. Before I knew it, I was speaking in London in front of 200 entrepreneurs about my book.

What has been your experience working with Gerry Robert?
Gerry is the best in the industry. If you're an aspiring author, your only option is to take action and use Gerry and his bootcamps. He and the Black Card Books team created a superstar system. They impeccably delivered all the tools I could have ever dreamed of to make my book happen. If you do your part, everything will fall into place.

Do you recommend the Publish a Book & Grow Rich bootcamp?
There were almost 1,000 people in Romania when Gerry came here. They were blown away. I was, too.

Geraldine Isa-al

Author of *Home At Last!*
Accountant

Email: geeisaal@gmail.com
Website: www.wealthstewardess.com
Visit my website for a FREE consultation on how you can be your own money manager.

What is your Primary Objective?
To boost sales for my business and create opportunities to share my ideas with as many people as possible. To reach Filipino migrant workers all over the world.

What has been your biggest win?
I've been able to spread my message to thousands of people and I've become known as an expert in my field.

What has been your experience working with Gerry Robert?
Two years ago, I made one of the greatest decisions in my life: I allowed myself to be mentored by the world changer himself, Gerry Robert. I've had to stretch myself and push way past my norms. I've had to become more resourceful and creative to bring my project to its full potential. It's been an awesome journey.

Do you recommend the Publish a Book & Grow Rich bootcamp?
I've been to all of the big seminar speakers and I can tell you, this one was one of the best (and biggest) I've attended. You must attend.

Ashikka Veerasamy

Author of *CHARGE Up Your Organization*
Author, Maverick, Change Artist

Email: ashikaveerasamy@icloud.com
Website: www.chargeupyourorg.com
Visit my website to receive a FREE one-hour business consultation.

What has been your biggest win?
My book was launched on April 20, 2016 – I applaud myself on the accomplishment of being a published author. The enthusiasm to share the view that economic sustainability relies on more than plain financials remains unbridled.

What has been your experience working with Gerry Robert?
Like walking a path with a trusted friend. A friend with a blueprint for mastery of the craft and the realization of dreams. Gerry Robert is the legendary dream-catcher of the publishing world. I am truly proud to be associated with him. What a visionary!

Do you recommend the Publish a Book & Grow Rich bootcamp?
I found it so helpful. Gerry gives EVERYTHING you need to get published fast and, more importantly, how to get the right book to build your business and income.

Kenneth Low

Author of *Family Legacy*
Author, Associate Estate Planner

Email: kennethlow@familylegacy.sg
Website: www.familylegacy.sg
Visit my website to receive a FREE 60-minute consultation on Will & Estate Planning.

What is your Primary Objective?
I'm using my book to market my legacy planning expertise and service to professionals and other high net worth clients. I plan to market myself as the go-to person for estate planning in my country.

What has been your biggest win?
I've got new ideas to market my service, doors opening in the area of networking, and great collaborations with others, leading to more and more market opportunities.

What has been your experience working with Gerry Robert?
Gerry and Black Card Books have a great support team that helps keep you on schedule. They're always encouraging me in my journey to finish the book.

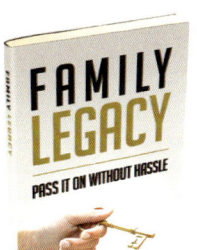

Do you recommend the Publish a Book & Grow Rich bootcamp?
I was amazed at the level of content and the sheer volume of strategies. I tell everyone to go to this one.

Mahesh Rajamani

Author of ENGAGEMENT
Author, Speaker, Entrepreneur

Email: mayat.mahesh@gmail.com
Website: www.maheshrajamani.com
Visit my website to receive a FREE coaching session.

What is your Primary Objective?
My book will lead to paid speaking engagements where I can spread my knowledge on taking products to the market.

What has been your biggest win?
The Instant Author Program has helped me focus on my business strategy. It has boosted my self-confidence to a height I've never reached before!

What has been your experience working with Gerry Robert?
Gerry and the team at Black Card Books are a source of tremendous inspiration. Getting my book published is a dream come true.

Do you recommend the Publish a Book & Grow Rich bootcamp?
What we loved the most was the FUND IT section where he showed us how to bring in $30,000 before we write a single word.

Dr. Iqbal K M

Author of UNLIMITED INCOME NOW
Doctor

Email: fabulous620@gmail.com
Website: www.learnfromexperts.net
Like my Facebook page at www.facebook.com/unlimitedincomenow to get FREE stock trading ideas, proven strategies for success in stocks, Forex and Indices from the top traders.

What is your Primary Objective?
I would like to meet world-renowned speakers who can improve the income of the audience by sharing their expertise. I would like the book to give me the credibility to organize their seminars.

What has been your biggest win?
As an author I get more credibility, respect and fame than what I got as a medical doctor. I've also met top trading champions who've shared techniques which have dramatically improved my trading skills and income. Now I can call them on the phone whenever I like.

What has been your experience working with Gerry Robert?
I've known Gerry Robert since 1995 when he was teaching *Money Mastery*. Gerry is a kind-hearted, witty man who wants to help everyone. His team of wonderful people really know what they're doing. They will help and support anyone to bring out the great book within them. Well done.

Do you recommend the Publish a Book & Grow Rich bootcamp?
If you are interested in a STEP-BY-STEP plan, then this is it.

Malik Jaffer

Author of *The Mobilizer*™
Author, Mobile Marketer

Email: malik@themobilizerguru.com
Website: www.themobilizerguru.com
Contact me to receive a FREE copy of my book and a 30-minute Mobile Marketing Consultation.

What is your Primary Objective?
To attain financial freedom, gain credibility and increase sales.

What has been your biggest win?
Opening doors to new and exciting partnerships. My book creates an enriched and diversified lead generation stream and gives me amazing international consultation opportunities.

What has been your experience working with Gerry Robert?
Gerry Robert and the Black Card Books team are a fine-tuned machine! They've been there for me every step of the way. Gerry's personal input and insights have helped me monetize aspects of my business I'd never thought of before.

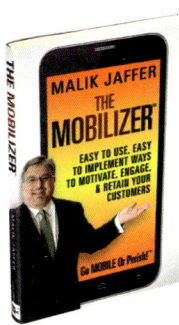

Do you recommend the Publish a Book & Grow Rich bootcamp?
In a day of high-pressure seminars where all they want to do is sell you their next course, this workshop had none of that crap. Nothing but solid content here.

Cat Martin

Author of *Gotta Love 'Em*
College Professor, Author

Email: cat@gottaloveem.com
Website: www.gottaloveem.com/Book
Visit my website to receive a FREE downloadable copy of my book.

What is your Primary Objective?
To help children who have experienced early childhood trauma heal by educating teachers. To have a voice as an expert in parenting children who have experienced trauma. Open doors for paid speaking invitations.

What has been your biggest win?
I've been invited to speak at three conferences and I'm getting two articles published. My book isn't even written yet!

What has been your experience working with Gerry Robert?
My one-on-one Skype meeting with Gerry transformed my simple idea of parents sharing their healing strategies with professionals and took it to a new level. He suggested options I hadn't considered. The whole Black Card Books team is there to help me succeed. I couldn't do this without them.

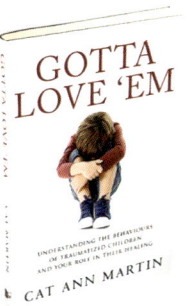

Do you recommend the Publish a Book & Grow Rich bootcamp?
5 STARS!!!

Tamsin Lancaster

Author of *I'm Fine*
Author, Speaker, YouTuber, Student

Email: imfine.book@gmail.com
Website: www.ImFine-Book.com
Contact me to receive a FREE autographed copy of my book and one FREE 30-minute consultation.

What is your Primary Objective?
To be a speaker. To be the voice for all teenagers across the world. I want to get the word out there and help teens everywhere. My book will bring great publicity for my YouTube channel.

What has been your biggest win?
Meeting the Mayor of my city and having her ask if she can help promote my book for me.

What has been your experience working with Gerry Robert?
The Black Card Books team is very supportive and with you every step of the way. The system is very professional but still easy to use.

Do you recommend the Publish a Book & Grow Rich bootcamp?
Mind-blowing!

Sue Curr

Author of *Fearless, Fierce & Fabulous*
Motivational Speaker

Email: suecurr@suecurrauthor.com
Website: www.suecurr.com
Visit my website to claim your FREE 30-minute Motivational Discovery Call.

What is your Primary Objective?
To build and sustain a high-end Motivational Speaker/Mentor business, providing me with multiple income streams. Enabling both an abundant and limitless lifestyle for me and my family.

What has been your biggest win?
Fearless, Fierce & Fabulous has opened the door for me to enter into negotiations that are leading to seeing one of my life-long dreams come to pass; it is very exciting and rewarding!

What has been your experience working with Gerry Robert?
The support and mentoring I've received from Gerry and the whole team has, in and of itself, been nothing less than inspirational; there is always someone to turn to for advice and guidance, and nothing is ever considered too small a concern to be important.

I really do feel part of the Black Card Books family.

Do you recommend the Publish a Book & Grow Rich bootcamp?
I couldn't give it higher praise.

Tony Dovale

Author of *SWIFT Success and The Action Ensurance Playbook*
Coach, Consultant

Website: www.swiftsuccessbook.com, www.successactivators.com
Visit my website to receive a FREE downloadable copy of my book.

What is your Primary Objective?
Build Wealth - Long Term. Build visibility, credibility, more talks, on LEADERSHIP and the REVOLUTIONARY WORKPLACE. Travel globally. Create residual income streams.

What has been your biggest win?
This Instant Author Program brought greater focus, clarity and vision to my work. As a result, I've taken action and transformed my wisdom into a brand identity I can share with a larger audience.

What has been your experience working with Gerry Robert?
Gerry Robert is the real deal. He's honest and authentic. In a world of plastic promises, he's genuine and forthright. His commitment, compassion and kindness are an inspiration. His positive mindset

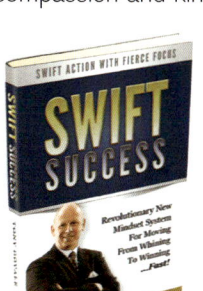

is a shining example to everyone he meets. He is THE global expert who will get you to your goals faster through his publishing and marketing excellence.

Do you recommend the Publish a Book & Grow Rich bootcamp?
I've presented on his stages and I am really picky about who I endorse, but I do so with Gerry without hesitation.

Dale Torgerson

Author of *SUCCEED With Oracle Hyperion Planning And Essbase*
Consultant

Email: dale@daletorgerson.com
Website: www.daletorgerson.com
Visit my website to receive a FREE Oracle Hyperion Planning and Essbase check-up checklist.

What is your Primary Objective?
To enhance my value as a Software Consultant.

What has been your biggest win?
I've learned that I can reach a much bigger audience with my skills and my message.

What has been your experience working with Gerry Robert?
Gerry's team at Black Card Books is a tremendous resource. They know how to pull all the pieces together to get the book done!

Do you recommend the Publish a Book & Grow Rich bootcamp?
Only to serious marketers who want a complete road map to success.

Nomer Meteoro

Author of *The Engine Of Success*
Author, President

Email: nomeronepositive@gmail.com
Website: www.theengineofsuccessbook.com
Visit my website to receive a FREE one-on-one mentoring session.

What is your Primary Objective?
This book will lead to speaking engagements and I hope it can be a blessing to others.

What has been your biggest win?
My self-worth. People always come to me for advice.

What has been your experience working with Gerry Robert?
Greatest experience in my life. Gerry is my mentor and role model.

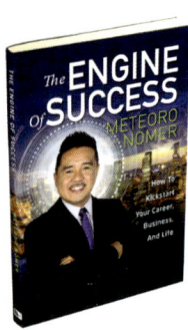

Do you recommend the Publish a Book & Grow Rich bootcamp?
When you attend something like this, you are often hesitant, not sure of what will happen. Well, what happened was nothing short of miraculous. I'll never be the same since attending this workshop. I implore you to get to it as soon as possible.

Becca Teers

Author of *UNLIMITED*
Author, Cognitive Behavioural Hypnotherapist

Email: b.teers@googlemail.com
Website: www.healthy-habits.me
Visit my website to receive a FREE one-hour Mindset Transformation Session.

What is your Primary Objective?
To expand my clientele for my private practice, increase participation in my Unlimited Workshops series and build sales for all of my online products and courses.

What has been your biggest win?
My upcoming book has already helped me to get valuable PR, which has helped market my business and services.

What has been your experience working with Gerry Robert?
My experience so far has been awesome. Gerry and the whole Black Card Books team have years of experience and knowledge in helping people write, publish and market their books.

Do you recommend the Publish a Book & Grow Rich bootcamp?
What a blast!!! I've told everyone about it. The smart ones attend.

Florin Pasat

Author of *WOW Now!*
Author, Speaker, Entrepreneur

Website: www.thewownowbook.com,
www.wownowbook.com
Visit www.thewownowbook.com for a FREE downloadable version of my book, *Wow Now!*, and visit www.wownowbook.com to receive a FREE download of The Inner Thermostat - Your Key To Wealth.

What is your Primary Objective?
To bring more clients to my workshops, develop my coaching program, and get more speaking engagements.

What has been your biggest win?
The biggest Romanian MLM company invited me to speak, which opened the door for me to work with them as a business consultant. My book and my workshops are now promoted through the organization's members.

What has been your experience working with Gerry Robert?
Gerry knows those tiny little things that make the difference between failure and success. He's eager to kindly share them with anyone who asks. The video testimonial he gave me instantly increased my conversion and my sales. Thank you, thank you, thank you!

Do you recommend the Publish a Book & Grow Rich bootcamp?
I've attended it numerous times. It's world-class. I'm a seminar speaker and I can assure you, you will love this bootcamp.

Jill Javelosa

Author of *The Handbook For Busy Parents*
Author, Early Literacy Specialist

Email: info@jillalvarez.com
Website: www.jillalvarez.com
Visit my website to choose your FREE 30-minute consultation on raising strong readers or writing a quality children's book.

What is your Primary Objective?
To teach minds, touch hearts and transform lives. I'd like my book to educate, inspire and empower others. I'd like to create a passive income stream so I can spend more time with my young children and use the income to serve others.

What has been your biggest win?
My biggest win is being able to connect with experts in my field and to be seen as an expert myself.

What has been your experience working with Gerry Robert?
The mentorship provided by Gerry Robert and Black Card Books is phenomenal. I'm confident and grateful knowing I'm working with people who treat my book as their own. They're passionate, knowledgeable and committed to bringing my vision to fruition.

Do you recommend the Publish a Book & Grow Rich bootcamp?
Just look at the agenda… PLAN IT, WRITE IT, PUBLISH IT, FUND IT, MOVE IT. It's all there for the taking.

Jack Mamo

Author of *The Marriage Code Book*
Premarital and Marriage Consultant

Email: Jack.mamo@live.ca
Website: www.themarriagecode.net
Visit my website to receive a FREE 30-minute relationship consultation.

What is your Primary Objective?
To create a lot of publicity for the marriage consulting service I provide for my clients.

What has been your biggest win?
My book has not even been printed yet and I've already started working with a well-known magazine publisher. He's ready to connect me with some very well-known Christian leaders, which I hope will be a huge success.

What has been your experience working with Gerry Robert?
Gerry and the Black Card Books team run like a well-oiled machine. They go out of their way to help no matter what. They lead you through whatever happens, politely but firmly encouraging you 'till you succeed. They're the best in the business; they serve you with honesty and integrity. What more can you ask for? I love working with them.

Do you recommend the Publish a Book & Grow Rich bootcamp?
Life changing, that's what it's like.

Maggie Georgopoulos

Author of *Up the Ladder in a Skirt*
Author, Speaker, Consultant

Email: maggie@uptheladderinaskirt.com
Website: www.uptheladderinaskirt.com
Purchase my book and receive a FREE pass to my 6-week online leadership course!

What is your Primary Objective?
To position myself as an authority in my field and get my business in front of more potential clients. To build, connect and grow my business toward sustainability and achieve the goals I see and know are possible!

What has been your biggest win?
I've increased my business worth and reach threefold in only three months – and my book hasn't even been published yet!

What has been your experience working with Gerry Robert?
Working with Gerry is an amazing learning experience. He's an energetic powerhouse with one of the fastest business brains I've ever seen. He can look at an idea and see the path to a seven-figure business in a matter of minutes.

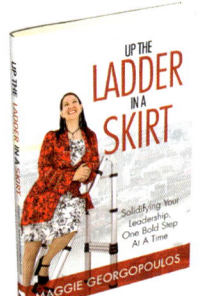

Do you recommend the Publish a Book & Grow Rich bootcamp?
If you miss this, you'll kick yourself forever. It's a blast and it'll get you published fast.

THE ROSE OF SHARON SCHOOL

Rose of Sharon Elementary School
is a caring school located in the slums on the outskirts of Barranquilla, Colombia.

Your support and generosity will get kids off the street and provide:

UNIFORMS
SCHOOL SUPPLIES
SCHOLARSHIPS
BREAKFAST AND LUNCH
A FIRST CLASS EDUCATION

BECOME A SPONSOR TODAY

You can give a child the opportunity to go to school, access to clean water, health care and nutrition.

Scan this code or call our office +1 877 280 8536 to find out how.
www.publishabookandgrowrich.com/rose

Get 2 FREE* Tickets

Let speaking legend **GERRY ROBERT**, who has spoken to 3 million people and generated over $200 million, show you how to...

USE A BOOK AS A MARKETING TOOL

THIS IS ABOUT... Aligning yourself with **GERRY ROBERT**. Branding yourself and your business. Attracting prospects like a magnet. Building your business the Gerry Robert way. Instantly gaining EXPERT status. Generating thousands of dollars within a month. Creating massive publicity.

ATTRACTION... Making prospects come directly to you.
DISTINCTION... Being different than everyone else.
VISIBILITY... Becoming a media personality.

AUTHORITY... Creating higher profits through smart positioning.
LONGEVITY... Ensuring shelf life for your efforts.
CREDIBILITY... Branding yourself as an expert.

Attend the Publish a Book & Grow Rich bootcamp. Over 100 are conducted per year, worldwide.

www.publishabookandgrowrich.com/freeticket

*Not applicable in every country.